IMAM MAHDI

HIS POSITION AND HIS MISSION

Shaykh Mohammad Saeed Bahmanpour
Edited and annotated by Mirza Muhammad Hasan Pooya

بسم الله الرحمن الرحيم

In the Name of God, the Beneficient, the Merciful

Published by
Sun Behind The Cloud Publications Ltd
PO Box 15889, Birmingham, B16 6NZ
This first edition published in 2023
Copyright Mohammad Saeed Bahmanpour 2023©
The moral right of the author has been asserted
All rights reserved
A CIP catalogue record of this book is available
from the British Library
ISBN (print): 978-1-908110-88-6
ISBN (ebook): 978-1-908110-89-3

www.sunbehindthecloud.com
info@sunbehindthecloud.com
Instagram: @sunbehindcloud
Facebook: @sunbehindthecloud

To the Remaining Guide of the Guides of Allah, Baqiyyatullah, whom we await to manifest himself and fill the earth with justice and equity after its prolonged period of inequity and cruelty.

Preface

The book in front of you is not the first book compiled about the Mahdi and will not be the last. It is a humble attempt to bring this seminal concept in Muslim theology to the attention of the English-speaking world from the perspective of the followers of the Ahlul Bayt. However, references will be made to discussions from other Muslim schools of thought where relevant. I will attempt to analyse the main foundations of this crucial concept and clarify some of the misunderstandings about his person, his position, and his mission that generally permeate these discussions.

The original contents of the book are transcriptions of some of my lectures on the topic delivered in 2015, the recordings of which were provided by Sarfraz Manji to whom we owe great thanks. I am also profusely grateful to Amineh Pooya who transcribed the recordings painstakingly despite her many other commitments. Similarly, I am grateful to Tehseen Merali from Sun Behind The Cloud Publications, as always, who did a magnificent job copyediting the whole text and making vital suggestions for improving the contents.

Last but not least, I appreciate the crucial contribution of Mirza Muhammad Hasan Pooya for editing the whole text, adding contents, and providing essential notes. Admittedly, this book would not have been possible without his enthusiasm and his tireless efforts.

And, above all, thanks to God, our maker and creator, who has assisted us with life, reason and provision to be able to accomplish what we accomplish.

Contents

Introduction

Part One – His Position   12

    Divine Guidance & Human Purpose   14
    The Guides and the Guided   16
    The *Muqarrabun*   17
    The Treasurers of Knowledge   19
    Hukm   21
    Khalifatullah   25
    Knowledge of The Names (*asma'*)   32
    The Warner and The Guide   36
    The Concept of Imam in The Qur'an   39
    The Concepty of the *Hujjah* (proof)   46
    The Continuity of the *Hujjah* (proof)   47
    Accessibility to The *Hujjah* (proof)   49
    The Twelve Successors   55
    The Twelve *Muhaddath*   58
    Muhaddath and *Siddiq*   62
    The Identity of The Ahlul Bayt   66
    A Summary of the Discussion so far   72
    The Identity of The Mahdi   73
    Traditions About the Occultation   76

Part Two - His Mission	**80**
A Contextual Perspective	81
Establishing The Book of God	82
The Defining Features of His Time	84
1. Justice	88
2. Increase in Faith and Reduction in Sin	90
3. Affluence	92
4. Security	97
5. The Growth of Knowledge	98
6. One Faith	100
7. Prevalence of Peace	102
8. Universal Altruism	102
9. Care for Nature	103
10. Enhancement of Life	103
Active Hope for The Ease (*faraj*)	104
Part Three - Our Responsibility in His Absence	**107**
The Leading Imam	108
Keeping Faith in Mahdi During His Absence	111
Merits of Expectation (*intidhar*)	113
The *Faraj* (ease)	117
In Preparation for His Coming	121
Endnotes	**126**

Introduction

Most religions have specific beliefs about the changes in the world that will occur at the end of time; each drawing comfort and optimism from the hope of a final saviour of humanity who will come to right wrongs, remove discord, and manifest the truth for what it really is.

The concept of a saviour has manifested throughout human history in the form of divinely appointed individuals. As awaited saviours in their times, Prophet Yusuf brought the Children of Israel from a little-known position to prominence. Prophet Musa delivered the Israelites to freedom after two centuries of enslavement. The long-anticipated Prophet Isa came to confront the corruption that had begun to pollute the practices of the Israelites; Prophet Muhammad - the Seal of the Prophets - represented the struggle and accomplishments of all the prophets before him. He was the fulfilment of the prophecies of Prophet Musa and Prophet Isa and it was in anticipation of his coming that different groups within the Israelites settled around Medina.

However, there is one final saviour who is expected by all. For centuries, the Muslims have been waiting for Mahdi, the Christians have been awaiting the return of Christ, whilst Jews await their redeemers in the Messiah, son of Joseph and the Messiah, son of David. Zoroastrians anticipate Saoshyant, Buddhists focus on Maitreya and Hindus rest their hopes in Kalki, the final avatar of Vishnu. One might be justified in wondering whether there is a common thread between these various traditions and if these religions are, in fact, waiting for the same person or set of connected events interpreted differently.

While commonalities between religions may be intriguing and provide the basis for dialogue, the purpose of this book is to understand this important belief in a saviour from the perspective of the Qur'an, Prophetic traditions, and the validation of the infallible Imams from the Ahlul Bayt. As we will see in these pages, according to these sources, the Mahdi's position and mission is not as a saviour for any particular religion, sect or nation; rather, he is the saviour and guide for all of humankind. He is the one awaited by all, though in different names and with different interpretations.

The concept of the Mahdi is entrenched within the Qur'anic idea of all-inclusive guidance and the notion of divine leadership (*imamah*). The following set of verses is only an example of the verses which have been accepted by the overwhelming majority of the scholars of the Qur'an as referring to a final saviour from the lineage of Prophet Muhammad.

وَلَقَدْ كَتَبْنَا فِي الزَّبُورِ مِنْ بَعْدِ الذِّكْرِ أَنَّ الْأَرْضَ يَرِثُهَا عِبَادِيَ الصَّالِحُونَ ۞

إِنَّ فِي هَذَا لَبَلَاغًا لِقَوْمٍ عَابِدِينَ وَمَا أَرْسَلْنَاكَ إِلَّا رَحْمَةً لِلْعَالَمِينَ ۞

And verily we have written in the Psalms, after the Scripture: My righteous slaves will inherit the earth.[1] Verily in this is a Message for people who would (truly) worship God. And We have not sent you but as a mercy to all people. (21:105-107)

These verses refer to a divine promise made in earlier scriptures about a saviour that is to be realised in the distant future. Prophet Muhammad spoke with emphasis about the advent of this saviour in the person of Mahdi before the end of time and the circumstances surrounding his coming. This led to the Mahdi becoming a dominant figure in Islamic discourse after the demise of the Prophet, regardless of sects and denominations. It was substantiated by *mutawatir* narrations. A *mutawatir* narration is one that has been reported so widely from diverse sources, that its contents are considered beyond doubt.[2]

That is why there is unanimous agreement and belief about the concept of the Mahdi among Muslim scholars.[3] Scholars with different persuasions have authored books exclusively on traditions regarding the Mahdi for over a thousand years. In fact, the 10th Hijri Islamic scholar, al Muttaqi al Hindi, in his book, *al Burhan fi Alamat Mahdi Aakhir al Zaman,* collated and quoted *fatawa* from the leaders of all four traditional schools of the time in Makkah—who were his contemporaries—regarding the Mahdi, indicating that this belief is one of the necessities of Islamic faith.[4]

Al Hindi reproduced their fatwas indicating that all of them believed in the *tawatur* of the traditions about the Mahdi, considering it as one of the 'necessary tenets' of Islam and stating that those who deny it are out of Muslim faith.

The first book ever written on the subject—that we know of—is *al Fitan wa al Malahim* (Trials and Tribulations) by the famous scholar, Hafiz Nu'aym ibn Hammad al Marwazi (d. 227 AH). He was the first scholar to author a *musnad* in the Sunni tradition and was one of the authorities of Bukhari and other authors of *sahih* books. He was also a contemporary of Imam al Reza and Imam al Jawad.[5]

Among Shia scholars, the first book recorded about the Mahdi is *al Ghaibah* by Fadl ibn Shadhan al Nayshaburi (d. 260 AH). He was a companion of Imam al Jawad, Imam al Hadi and Imam al Askari. Interestingly, he narrated traditions about the occultation long before the event. This book is no longer in existence, and we only know of it from bibliographical indexes.

Thereafter, books were written exclusively on the Mahdi in every century by both Shia and Sunni scholars.[6]

In the epilogue to *Sharh al Maqasid*, the well-known Ash'ari theologian, Sa'd al Din al Taftazani (d. 793 AH) writes:

> Related to the chapter on Imamah, is the emergence of the Mahdi and the descent of Isa, and they are among the portents of the Hour...It is reported from Abu Saeed al Khudri, may God be pleased with him, that he said: "The Messenger of God mentioned a calamity that would afflict this nation so that a man would not find an asylum to take refuge in it from injustice. Then, God would send a man from his family, and he will fill the earth with equity and justice as it was filled with oppression and tyranny." Scholars have suggested that he is simply an imam from the descendants of Fatima, may God be pleased with her. God will create him when He Wills and send him to support His religion.
>
> The Imami Shias presume that he is Muhammad ibn al Hasan al Askari who hid from the people for fear of enemies; they believe that there was no impossibility in his long life like Noah, Luqman and al Khidr, peace be upon them. However other sects denied that because they claim it is extremely unlikely, as no such ages are known in this nation and there is no conclusive evidence to support this claim.

This statement demonstrates that although there is some dispute over the identity of the Mahdi, there is little dispute amongst Muslim scholars in the concept of the Mahdi and the belief that he will arrive.

PART ONE
HIS POSITION

The spiritual position of the twelve Imams has been a topic of much debate in the Muslim community through the ages. It has led to certain false assumptions and sects being created even amongst Shias because of this element of confusion among the masses.

While the Sunni school of thought does not subscribe to belief in *imamah* as an institution of inspired knowledge, within the Shia school there has been a spectrum of opinions regarding the spiritual position of the Imam. At one end of this spectrum are those who claim that the Imams were simply pious, righteous, and knowledgeable scholars; or as they call them *al ulama al abrar*, Righteous Scholars. Their belief is very similar to the Sunni idea about the Imams of the Ahlul Bayt who accept their status as the household of the Prophet, and accept that they were knowledgeable and noble, but they claim that the Imams were merely scholarly jurists (*al ulama al mujtahidun*), who deduced their knowledge from the Holy Book and *sunnah* of the Prophet like any other learned person.

At the other end of the spectrum are the exaggerators, *ghulat*, who say that the Imams are themselves divine, attributing God-like qualities to them, for example, by claiming that sustenance (*rizq*) comes from them directly. They attribute *al siffaat al uluhiyyah* to the Imams, which are attributes that exclusively belong to God, including the ability to make decisions about the world, the management of affairs and similar matters which fall exclusively in the domain of Lordship (*rububiyyah*).

However, the Imams are reported to have said, "*See us as created servants, then whatever good you attribute to about us would be right.*"[7] This means that attributing a characteristic to the Imams that exclusively belongs to God is unacceptable and is an exaggeration. Both ends of the spectrum of *ghali* (exaggerator) and *muqassir* (falling short) —those unnecessarily raising the status of the Imams or those degrading their status — are not considered part of mainstream Shia thought. Of course, people are entitled to their opinions, but there is a standard based on the Qur'an, *sunnah* and the sayings of the Imams themselves and one must remain careful not to follow either extreme.

The mainstream Shia belief is that while the Imams certainly do not have divine attributes, they are divinely-inspired in their knowledge and actions. They do not derive their knowledge from books like ordinary *mujtahideen* (jurists).

Mujtahideen have the status of the *maraaji'*. They gain knowledge through studying and researching. None of them are inspired (in the proper sense of the word) in their knowledge, and that is why their religious directives are sufficient only for the fulfilment of duty and not as certain knowledge. Most people do not possess high levels of juristic knowledge, so they have to follow a person who has acquired that level of knowledge, and this is their argument before God if they are asked why the behaved in certain manner. However, the *maraaji'* are not a *hujjah* (proof) in the sense of being the ultimate knowledge whose words are the word of God.

The mainstream Shia standpoint is somewhere in the middle of the continuum; the Imams are not divine beings as the *ghulat* (exaggerators) have offered, but they are above *al ulema al mujtahidoon* (jurist scholars).

If the Imam is to be the proof (*hujjah*) and the guide for every age, his knowledge needs to be divinely-inspired, otherwise he rationally cannot be a true proof from God. In the absence of this inspired knowledge there would be no difference between him and other scholars nor would he possess spiritual authority over the believers. This is also the characteristic the Qur'an upholds for a true Imam:

وَجَعَلْنَاهُمْ أَئِمَّةً يَهْدُونَ بِأَمْرِنَا وَأَوْحَيْنَا إِلَيْهِمْ فِعْلَ الْخَيْرَاتِ وَإِقَامَ الصَّلَاةِ

$$\text{وَإِيتَاءَ الزَّكَاةِ وَكَانُوا لَنَا عَابِدِينَ}$$

And We made them Imams who guided (people) by Our command, and We revealed to them the doing of good and the keeping up of prayer and the giving of the alms, and Us (alone) did they serve; (21:73)

Thus in this section, we will seek to understand the spiritual position of the Mahdi according to the mainstream Shia thought. This will be through elucidating certain concepts related to the position of the Imams including Imam Mahdi, such as being a Guide (*hadi*) being among 'those who are drawn close' (*muqarrabun*), possessing 'final verdict' (*hukm*), their role as 'the representative of God' (*khalifatullah*) and 'the proof of God' (*hujjatullah*), among other concepts that will unfold during the course of the section.

Divine Guidance and the fulfilment of Human Purpose

The purpose of the human race in this phase of life is to know and worship God as the only means to their growth and self-development. It is stated in the Qur'an that:

$$\text{وَمَا خَلَقْتُ الْجِنَّ وَالْإِنْسَ إِلَّا لِيَعْبُدُونِ}$$

I did not create the jinn and the humans except that they may worship Me. (51:56)

What this worship means and what it necessitates requires knowledge and understanding given that we are conscious beings with freedom of choice. Worship cannot be intentionally exercised without knowledge, and that knowledge must be present somewhere. Surah Saffat states that it is with the purified servants of God:

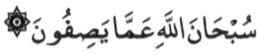

$$\text{إِلَّا عِبَادَ اللَّهِ الْمُخْلَصِينَ}$$

Clear is God of whatever they allege [about Him]
—[all] except God's exclusive servants. (37:159-160)

The verses suggest that God cannot be directly fathomed by ordinary human minds; we may make grave mistakes if left to our own thoughts and imaginations. We may anthropomorphise God, attribute false notions to Him, assume partners for Him or we may deny His existence altogether. It is only the chosen and purified among human race who can speak of God with truth and accuracy. This requires a high degree of knowledge that is granted to them by God Himself.

$$\text{أَفَمَن يَهْدِي إِلَى الْحَقِّ أَحَقُّ أَن يُتَّبَعَ أَمَّن لَّا يَهِدِّي إِلَّا أَن يُهْدَىٰ ۖ فَمَا لَكُمْ كَيْفَ تَحْكُمُونَ}$$

Is he who guides to the truth worthier to be followed, or he who is not guided unless shown the way? What is the matter with you? How do you judge? (10:35)

Although believers are inclined to have deep feelings of faith in their hearts, they often do not have true knowledge of God. Clear and deep understanding is only placed in the hearts of the purified servants of God who are the divine guides.

In this way, divine guides play a crucial role in fulfilling the purpose of mankind on earth.

Without them, our existence would be rendered futile; humanity would be crushed under the heel of the destructive tendencies inherent in our material makeup. It is only when we are guided through the path of controlling material tendencies combined with a higher spiritual sense of self and movement towards an ordained direction, that we can actualise the purpose of our creation.

This is also why the knowledge and guidance these guides bring must continuously exist on Earth—in order to preserve the connection between man and his creator. Many narrations state that if this knowledge is withdrawn from the earth, then the purpose of man's creation would be in vain and the earth would swallow its inhabitants.

Someone asked Imam al Sadiq, *"Would the earth remain without the Imam?"* He replied, *"Should the earth remain without the Imam it would sink in."*[8]

The Guides and the Guided

When Prophet Adam and his wife Hawwaa were informed that they had to live on earth, they were promised that there would be no fear for them or their progeny as long as they followed the guidance sent to them by God.

قُلْنَا اهْبِطُوا مِنْهَا جَمِيعًا فَإِمَّا يَأْتِيَنَّكُم مِّنِّي هُدًى فَمَن تَبِعَ هُدَايَ فَلَا خَوْفٌ عَلَيْهِمْ وَلَا هُمْ يَحْزَنُونَ ۞

We said, "Get down from it, all together! Yet, should any guidance come to you from Me, those who follow My guidance shall have no fear, nor shall they grieve." (2:38)

This guidance came in the form of revelation to some members of the progeny of Adam. It was these members of the same seed who had to guide others, not any angel or supernatural being. Thus, from the beginning of the history of man on earth, there were individuals chosen by God to guide people. The Qur'an reveals the identity of some of these guides:

إِنَّ اللَّهَ اصْطَفَىٰ آدَمَ وَنُوحًا وَآلَ إِبْرَاهِيمَ وَآلَ عِمْرَانَ عَلَى الْعَالَمِينَ ۞

Indeed, God chose Adam and Noah, and the progeny of Ibrahim and the progeny of Imran above all the nations. (3:33)

Those who were chosen to guide had qualities bestowed to them by God that others did not possess. They had to be extremely pure and sincere, to be able to serve as a receptacle of the knowledge of God and a conduit to convey His message to the people. They were not 'super-humans' but 'extra-pure humans', specially chosen with blessings granted to them by God to help them fulfil their roles as guides.

These were the prophets, who guided through revelation, and their successors, who were appointed by God to preserve the revealed message and interpret the Books after the prophets, all of whom were chosen from among the *muqarrabun*.

The *Muqarrabun*

From a religious vista, people are normally divided by the criterion of faith;into believers and disbelievers. However, the Qur'an categorises people into *three* groups; the believers, the disbelievers, and those who are drawn close [to God]—the *muqarrabun*. Although the latter group could also be regarded as an elite subsection of believers; they are crucially different from ordinary believers and are classified differently.

From one perspective, as mentioned, there are those among the believers who should be guided and those who guide, and although both groups are believers, they are never regarded as comparable.

أَفَمَنْ يَهْدِي إِلَى الْحَقِّ أَحَقُّ أَنْ يُتَّبَعَ أَمَّنْ لَا يَهِدِّي إِلَّا أَنْ يُهْدَىٰ فَمَا لَكُمْ كَيْفَ تَحْكُمُونَ ۞

Is He who guides to the truth worthier to be followed, or he who is not guided unless shown the way? What is the matter with you? How do you judge? (10:35.)

From another perspective, believers yearn to be guided to the path of certain believers like those referred to in the opening chapter of the Qur'an as *an'amta 'alayhim* (those whom You have favoured). These individuals are set as guides, signposts, and role models as the prayer in the opening chapter testifies:

اهْدِنَا الصِّرَاطَ الْمُسْتَقِيمَ ۚ صِرَاطَ الَّذِينَ أَنْعَمْتَ عَلَيْهِمْ ..

Guide us to the straight path, the path of those **whom You have favoured** (1:6-7)

At the first glance, one may think that those upon whom the favour of God is bestowed and those who are drawn close refers to the prophets who guide others without the need to be guided by anyone else. However, the following verse of the Qur'an gives a wider interpretation to this favoured group and extends it to some other ranks as well.

وَمَنْ يُطِعِ اللَّهَ وَالرَّسُولَ فَأُولَٰئِكَ مَعَ الَّذِينَ أَنْعَمَ اللَّهُ عَلَيْهِمْ مِنَ النَّبِيِّينَ وَالصِّدِّيقِينَ وَالشُّهَدَاءِ وَالصَّالِحِينَ ۚ وَحَسُنَ أُولَٰئِكَ رَفِيقًا ۞

Whoever obeys God and the Apostle they are with those whom God has favoured, including **the prophets** and **the truthful**, **the witnesses** and **the righteous**; and excellent companions are they. (4:69)

According to this verse, four groups of believers are favoured by God: the prophets, the truthful, the witnesses, and the righteous. Those who obey God and the Prophet are promised that they will be *with* the favoured ones, not *from* them but *with* them.

One possible meaning of 'drawing close to God' is to gain more knowledge about Him such that some veils are removed from the heart allowing the *muqarrabun* to feel His presence and to see and hear what ordinary believers are usually deprived of. This could be regarded as a big favour, which is not easily extended to all believers. According to Imam Ali, "*Such people are very few in number, but they are highly esteemed by God.*"[9] They come to an understanding of this world and a type of knowledge of its Creator that is genuinely different from others. "*They look at the inner side of this world while others look only at the outer side. God whispers in their minds and speaks with them in their very intellect and thus they kindle a light in others' hearts and ears and eyes.*"[10]

This is, in brief, the merit and position of the Imams: they are guides who have inspired knowledge; the type of knowledge that is preserved by them in this world carries forward into the next world. This is why in *Ziyarah al Jamiah al Kabirah*, they are called, *khuzzan al ilm*, the Treasurers of Knowledge.

The Treasurers of Knowledge

The Imam or divinely-appointed leader serves as the focal point where knowledge descends (after the Prophet), and the true and authentic connection between Man and God is preserved through him. If that connection is not preserved, life on earth would cease to continue. It is important to bear in mind that this discussion is not about the dissemination of knowledge at this point, but only the point of connection where this knowledge descends and is received.

The Holy Prophet was a teacher and interpreter of the revelation that he received.

$$\text{وَأَنزَلْنَا إِلَيْكَ ٱلذِّكْرَ لِتُبَيِّنَ لِلنَّاسِ مَا نُزِّلَ إِلَيْهِمْ وَلَعَلَّهُمْ يَتَفَكَّرُونَ}$$

We have revealed to you the Reminder that you may make clear to men what has been revealed to them, and that haply they may reflect. (16:44)

The Prophet also performed a limited number of miracles to convince people to follow the right way; for some this was sufficient, while others still turned away. Although the companions of the Prophet learnt how he prayed, how to behave, what to do and what to avoid, not all of them could comprehend the overwhelming knowledge of God that he had within his heart. There is a deep and special category of knowledge that can only be taught through the Holy Spirit rather than being learnt by experience. The following verses from the Holy Qur'an inform us that there is an elite, non-prophetic category of people whose exceptional knowledge and awareness makes them unwavering witnesses to the unique oneness of God, His Divine Justice, and the truthfulness of the Prophet. This deep-rooted knowledge accords them the status of authorised interpreters of the hidden and sublime verses of the Holy Qur'an, and the safeguards against misguidance after the Prophet.

شَهِدَ اللّٰهُ أَنَّهُ لَا إِلَٰهَ إِلَّا هُوَ وَالْمَلَائِكَةُ وَأُولُو الْعِلْمِ قَائِمًا بِالْقِسْطِ لَا إِلَٰهَ إِلَّا هُوَ الْعَزِيزُ الْحَكِيمُ ۞

God bears witness that there is no god except Him, and [so do] the angels **and those who possess knowledge,** maintaining His creation with justice; there is no god but He, the Mighty, the Wise. (3:18)

وَيَقُولُ الَّذِينَ كَفَرُوا لَسْتَ مُرْسَلًا قُلْ كَفَىٰ بِاللّٰهِ شَهِيدًا بَيْنِي وَبَيْنَكُمْ وَمَنْ عِنْدَهُ عِلْمُ الْكِتَابِ ۞

The faithless say, "You have not been sent [by God]." Say, "God suffices as a witness between me and you, and **he who possesses the knowledge of the Book.**" Qur'an 13:43

It is because of this very knowledge that God has appointed them as having the final word (*hukm*) in religious and spiritual matters.

Hukm

In the Qur'an, we find the usage of the word *hukm* when referring to a quality given to certain people. Exegetes have grappled with the exact meaning of this term when trying to explain various verses.

For example, in Surah Maryam, Prophet Yahya was given *hukm* as a child:

$$\text{يَا يَحْيَىٰ خُذِ ٱلْكِتَٰبَ بِقُوَّةٍ وَءَاتَيْنَٰهُ ٱلْحُكْمَ صَبِيًّا}$$

'O John!' [We said,] 'Hold on with power to the Book!' And We gave him *hukm* while still a child. (19:12)

In Surah Shu'ara, Prophet Ibrahim prayed to God for *hukm*;

$$\text{رَبِّ هَبْ لِي حُكْمًا وَأَلْحِقْنِي بِٱلصَّٰلِحِينَ}$$

My Lord! Grant me [unerring] *hukm*, and unite me with the Righteous. (26:83)

In the same surah, Prophet Musa explained to the Pharaoh that he had been given *hukm* when he fled from Egypt:

$$\text{فَفَرَرْتُ مِنكُمْ لَمَّا خِفْتُكُمْ فَوَهَبَ لِي رَبِّي حُكْمًا وَجَعَلَنِي مِنَ ٱلْمُرْسَلِينَ}$$

So I fled from you, as I was afraid of you. Then my Lord gave me *hukm* and made me one of the apostles. (26:21)

The term *hukm* has most commonly been translated as wisdom. This is also the general translation for *hikmah*, which comes from the same root word in Arabic but has a different meaning to *hukm*.

Prophet Musa's reply to the Pharaoh shows that the Qur'anic understanding of *hukm* signifies a mandate or judgement. This *hukm* given to Prophet Musa is also mentioned in another place in the Qur'an:

وَلَمَّا بَلَغَ أَشُدَّهُ وَاسْتَوَىٰ آتَيْنَاهُ حُكْمًا وَعِلْمًا ۚ وَكَذَٰلِكَ نَجْزِي الْمُحْسِنِينَ ۞

When he came of age and became fully matured, We gave him *hukm* and knowledge, and thus do We reward the virtuous. (28:14)

And in similar words for Prophet Yusuf:

وَلَمَّا بَلَغَ أَشُدَّهُ آتَيْنَاهُ حُكْمًا وَعِلْمًا ۚ وَكَذَٰلِكَ نَجْزِي الْمُحْسِنِينَ ۞

When he came of age, We gave him *hukm* and [sacred] knowledge, and thus do We reward the virtuous. (12:22)

In fact, *hukm* in the Qur'an is the authority to utter the final word about faith, about God and about the *sharia*. This final agency can only be given to a person with immense knowledge who is trusted by God.

Once a person with this *hukm* (authority) makes a claim on a matter, they must be obeyed.

وَمَا كَانَ لِمُؤْمِنٍ وَلَا مُؤْمِنَةٍ إِذَا قَضَى اللَّهُ وَرَسُولُهُ أَمْرًا أَن يَكُونَ لَهُمُ الْخِيَرَةُ مِنْ أَمْرِهِمْ ۗ وَمَن يَعْصِ اللَّهَ وَرَسُولَهُ فَقَدْ ضَلَّ ضَلَالًا مُّبِينًا ۞

A faithful man or woman may not have any option in a matter when God and His Apostle have decided on their matter, and whoever disobeys God and His Apostle has certainly strayed into manifest error. (33:36)

Over the ages, this authority was given to God's chosen servants at different stages in their lives. It was bestowed on Prophet Musa in adulthood, on Prophet Yusuf in his youth and Prophet Yahya was given the authority to talk about God whilst just a child. Similarly, Imam al Jawad and Imam al Hadi were given this *hukm* when they were children. Having *hukm* makes a person to be the proof or *hujjah* on the earth.

Thus, the *hujjah* on earth is a person who has the authority to have the definitive and final word about God, the Scripture, and about the philosophy of life and the afterlife. In contrast, the laws and the opinions of the *mujtahidoon* are continuously debated and iterated over time.

Ironically, our knowledge today about matters of faith, the Prophet and the Qur'an is much deeper, broadly speaking, than that of the people who lived at the time of the Prophet. Many perceive it to be otherwise, especially the Salafis who tend to prioritise the *Salaf* (earlier generations). The Salafi reasoning is that the best people in Islam are the companions of the Prophet, followed by the generation after them and so on, each of whom they consider as having a higher level of understanding than contemporary generations.

This viewpoint is not correct because, notwithstanding the inspiration that radiated from the presence of the Prophet, the general population at the time of the Prophet had a very rudimentary knowledge about matters of faith. They did not adequately understand the character of the Prophet nor suitably comprehend his position.

On the other hand, over the past 1400 years, we have assimilated, deeply reflected upon, discussed and debated Qur'anic verses and *hadith*. Therefore, with the benefit of these debates and hindsight, our knowledge of these verses is broader and more wholesome than the knowledge of some of the companions who actually met the Prophet. This is obviously excluding a minority of companions who excelled in knowledge and virtue. Hence it should not be naturally assumed that those in close physical proximity to the Prophet had the strongest faith or knowledge. In fact, many historic narrations report that when the Prophet directed the companions about an issue, they would ask, *"O' Prophet, is this revelation or is this your opinion?"* They remarked that if his words were revelation, they would obey but if they were his own words then they would challenge him.

Today we understand that there is no difference between the opinion of the Prophet and what was revealed to him, because he had *hukm,* and as such he was divinely-inspired to do good in every action, as the verse suggests: *We revealed to them the doing of good* (21:73). There is clearly a shortcoming among some quarters in understanding the proper position of the Prophet and the Imams. There was harmony in their words, actions, and every aspect of their existence was lived according to divine inspiration and guidance. As a result, whatever they did was good (*khair*). It was due to such a divinely inspired quality that they represented God on earth — they were *khalifatullah*.

Khalifatullah

Khalifa is often translated as 'Successor' 'Viceroy' or 'Vicegerent'. In Qur'anic terminology, there are three meanings given to *khalifa* according to the different contexts of the verses. In one context, it is stated that the human race are collectively the successors (*khulafa*). This is what is mentioned at the end of Surah Ana'm:

وَهُوَ ٱلَّذِى جَعَلَكُمْ خَلَٰٓئِفَ ٱلْأَرْضِ وَرَفَعَ بَعْضَكُمْ فَوْقَ بَعْضٍ دَرَجَٰتٍ لِّيَبْلُوَكُمْ فِى مَآ ءَاتَىٰكُمْ إِنَّ رَبَّكَ سَرِيعُ ٱلْعِقَابِ وَإِنَّهُۥ لَغَفُورٌ رَّحِيمٌ ۝

It is He who has made you successors on the earth and raised some of you in rank above others so that He may test you in respect to what He has given you. Indeed, your Lord is swift in retribution, and indeed, He is all-Forgiving, all-Merciful. (6:165)

The verse addresses humanity as a whole saying that God has made human beings His viceroys and raised some in rank above others so that He may test them with respect to what He has given them. Thus, collectively we are *khalifatullah* in the sense that we do things that God intended for us to do on Earth; we construct, make tools, plough the earth, harvest and even create things. This is a role that has been given to mankind. We have been given the ability to develop in ways that many used to think were limited to God alone. We have cloned plants and animals and our experiments with genetics are on the brink of tampering with human creation. In the future, we may well create human beings.

Some people may say simplistically that these actions are intruding on the realm of God and that if we were ever able to do this, we would become God. However, the reason we can do all this is because of being *khalifatullah* on earth. God endowed us with the faculties and prowess to achieve these feats. We may be able to do things that God can, but not in the *way* He does them. Our ability comes through experimentation and exploring our God-given knowledge.

Some individuals like Prophet Isa could heal incurable diseases and even revive the dead—actions usually associated with God. Ordinary people can heal as well, but with the help of science and medicine - not in a miraculous way, which utilises special faculties given by God. It is important to remember that humanity can use this knowledge for evil as well. We can be good *khalifutallah* or bad ones who misuse their position and faculties.

Even though many Qur'anic exegetes refer to *khalifa* as one nation succeeding the other, some, like Fakhr al din Razi (d. 606 AH), have alluded to this fact very intelligently. Fakhr al din Razi says: "*They are viceroys of God on the earth; they own it and avail themselves of it.*"[11] This means, they build on it, create things in it and make it a better place for living. This can be seen when we study our history as humanity. The rise of stunning civilizations across the world attests to the creative progress of man.

The second implication of *khalifah* is the succession of nations. God destroyed nations before us; we came after them and thus become their *khalifa*, their successors. This context of the word appears in several verses of the Qur'an, for example:

$$ثُمَّ جَعَلْنَاكُمْ خَلَائِفَ فِي الْأَرْضِ مِنْ بَعْدِهِمْ لِنَنْظُرَ كَيْفَ تَعْمَلُونَ$$

Then We made you successors on the earth after them that We may observe how you will act. (10:14)

In this verse, God qualifies this succession or inheritance as one to which responsibilities are attached i.e. to test action and performance.

The study of nations, races and previous generations is fascinating. Every nation has enjoyed huge power at one point or another in history. In the past, the Chinese, Persian, and Egyptian empires ruled the world; currently, the era belongs to the West—Europe and America—who, in turn, have risen from the ashes of the Greek and Roman Empires. Similarly, Africa and South America have had great civilisations and powerful empires. As the Qur'an explains, God is alternating this invalidated power between civilizations to test how humans behave.

وَتِلْكَ الْأَيَّامُ نُدَاوِلُهَا بَيْنَ النَّاسِ وَلِيَعْلَمَ اللَّهُ الَّذِينَ آمَنُوا وَيَتَّخِذَ مِنكُمْ شُهَدَاءَ وَاللَّهُ لَا يُحِبُّ الظَّالِمِينَ ۞

We make such vicissitudes rotate among mankind, so that God may ascertain those who have faith, and that He may take witnesses from among you, and God does not like the wrongdoers. (3:140)

This is based on the Divine Justice of God, in order that people do not complain later by saying that had they enjoyed authority they would have been better.

In Surah Al Ara'f the Prophet Hud says to his people:

وَعَجِبْتُمْ أَن جَاءَكُمْ ذِكْرٌ مِّن رَّبِّكُمْ عَلَىٰ رَجُلٍ مِّنكُمْ لِيُنذِرَكُمْ وَاذْكُرُوا إِذْ جَعَلَكُمْ خُلَفَاءَ مِن بَعْدِ قَوْمِ نُوحٍ وَزَادَكُمْ فِي الْخَلْقِ بَسْطَةً فَاذْكُرُوا آلَاءَ اللَّهِ لَعَلَّكُمْ تُفْلِحُونَ ۞

Do you consider it odd that there should come to you a reminder from your Lord through a man from among yourselves, so that he may warn you? Remember when He made you successors after the people of Nuh, and increased you vastly in creation. So remember God's bounties that you may be felicitous. (7:69)

This verse fits with both meanings of *khalifa* discussed so far; firstly, He made them His viceroys on Earth and secondly, He made them successors of the people who passed before them.

The third meaning of *khalifa* is the allusion specific to prophets and their spiritual successors. They are the representatives of God in their individual and untainted capacity and not in the general sense applied to mankind. We do not represent God in the way His ambassadors do, due to our tendency towards error and injustice.

يَا دَاوُدُ إِنَّا جَعَلْنَاكَ خَلِيفَةً فِي الْأَرْضِ فَاحْكُم بَيْنَ النَّاسِ بِالْحَقِّ وَلَا تَتَّبِعِ الْهَوَىٰ فَيُضِلَّكَ عَن سَبِيلِ اللَّهِ ۞

'O Dawud! Indeed, We have made you a vicegerent on the earth. So judge between people with justice, and do not follow your desires, or they will lead you astray from the way of God.' (38:26)

This verse in Surah Saad speaks to Prophet Dawud as God's vicegerent in his personal capacity and reminds him to decide between people with justice, implying that Prophet Dawud's judgement represents God's judgement. This is why Prophet Dawud is reminded not to base his actions on personal bias otherwise he would be straying from the mandate given to him by God. This verse exemplifies the high moral standards and absolute justice that the *khalifatullah* demonstrate.

One might ask: *What do the Prophets and Imams represent from God as His khulafa (vicegerents) on the earth?* The first aspect is that they guide people on His behalf; this guidance is not based on their personal preferences or desires. That is why the concept of *ismah* (purity from sin) is so closely associated with divinely-granted responsibility.

The basis for this guidance radiates from the knowledge granted by God. When Prophet Adam came down to this earth, he came with this knowledge, and it was then preserved in the proofs (*hujjaj*) and viceroys (*khulafa*) after him. These leaders use their special knowledge to guide and judge righteously and correctly; their thoughts, feelings, and actions represent God, not their own personal desires. If they become angry, it means God is angry; if they become happy, it means God is happy. This is what is meant by "they represent God". This concept is embedded within the texts of different 'salutations', including *Ziyarah al Jamiah al Kabirah*. "*O Friend of God! There stand between me and God, the Almighty and all-Majestic, sins that He would not demolish except by attaining your satisfaction.*"[12] The *khalifatullah* in this context holds the highest meaning of the term. Their pleasure represents His pleasure, their judgement represents His judgement, and their anger represents His anger.

Some people label this way of speaking as a type of shirk, while this is exactly the position God has given them, and is explicitly validated in the Qur'an:

$$إِنَّ الَّذِينَ يُؤْذُونَ اللَّهَ وَرَسُولَهُ لَعَنَهُمُ اللَّهُ فِي الدُّنْيَا وَالْآخِرَةِ وَأَعَدَّ لَهُمْ عَذَابًا مُهِينًا ۝$$

Indeed, those who offend God and His Apostle are cursed by God in the world and the Hereafter, and He has prepared a humiliating punishment for them. (33:57)

$$إِنَّ الَّذِينَ يُبَايِعُونَكَ إِنَّمَا يُبَايِعُونَ اللَّهَ يَدُ اللَّهِ فَوْقَ أَيْدِيهِمْ ۝$$

Indeed, those who swear allegiance to you, swear allegiance to Allah: the hand of Allah is above their hands. (48:10)

Similarly, after all the torment and trouble the Pharoah gave to Prophet Musa, God says:

$$فَلَمَّا آسَفُونَا انْتَقَمْنَا مِنْهُمْ فَأَغْرَقْنَاهُمْ أَجْمَعِينَ ۝$$

When at length they enraged Us, We exacted retribution from them, and We drowned them all. (43:55)

Regarding the above verse, someone asked Imam al Sadiq if it was possible for God to become enraged. He reasoned that such an emotion denotes excitement and movement, and God does not have human feelings, so what did *falamma aasafoona* (when at length they enraged us) mean? Imam al Sadiq replied that when they enraged Prophet Musa it was as if they enraged God because he was a representative of God on Earth.[13] This is why the pronoun is in the plural that they *enraged Us*. Therefore, the feelings of the *khalifa* represent God as do their behaviour and their practices.

God commands us repeatedly in the Qur'an to "*Obey God and His Messenger*". Obedience to God means following the instructions and advice in the Qur'an and obedience to the Messenger means that even when there is no revelation, God commands us to follow the Prophet in whatever he says. This is because God's command and will is personified through the Prophet whether it is through Qur'anic revelation or Prophetic narration. The Prophet's words and actions are always representative of God's will.

Bearing this in mind, it is rather strange that sometimes the companions would ask the Prophet whether what he had just said was his opinion or a revelation. The Qur'an says in Surah al Hashr:

وَمَا آتَاكُمُ الرَّسُولُ فَخُذُوهُ وَمَا نَهَاكُمْ عَنْهُ فَانتَهُوا ۚ وَاتَّقُوا اللَّهَ ۖ إِنَّ اللَّهَ شَدِيدُ الْعِقَابِ ۞

Take whatever the Apostle gives you and refrain from whatever he forbids you, and be wary of God. Indeed, God is severe in retribution. (59:7)

Whether what the Prophet instructs, commands, or exemplifies, is revelation or not, is irrelevant—he must be obeyed in every circumstance. This is because the Prophet does not speak or act, except by God's Will. He has been given the *hukm*, therefore, whatever he does is based on that wisdom, not any selfish desire or ambition.

This level of knowledge manifests in character and qualities, as a *khalifatullah* has many duties to discharge. One may argue that many people strive and remain within God's guidelines, but they are not considered *khalifatullah*. The difference lies in the quality of connection to God and the degree of submission to Him. Humans have varying degrees of submission. The highest degree is to prefer God over everything else, and to have a clear vision when it comes to the vanities and deceptions of the world - this is the true guideline. A person is said to be astray when he does not follow those guidelines that have been given by God.

فَإِن لَّمْ يَسْتَجِيبُوا لَكَ فَاعْلَمْ أَنَّمَا يَتَّبِعُونَ أَهْوَآءَهُمْ وَمَنْ أَضَلُّ مِمَّنِ ٱتَّبَعَ هَوَىٰهُ بِغَيْرِ هُدًى مِّنَ ٱللَّهِ ۚ إِنَّ ٱللَّهَ لَا يَهْدِى ٱلْقَوْمَ ٱلظَّٰلِمِينَ ۞

But if they do not answer you, then know that they only follow their low desires; and who is more erring than he who follows his low desires without any guidance from God? Surely God does not guide the unjust people. (28:50)

The important thing to remember is that a *khalifatullah* does not achieve this position of his own volition, nor does anyone else have a part in his appointment. It is God alone who selects His chosen guides. The primary characteristic of these guides is that they do not follow their own desires in any matter, their judgement is God's judgement, and their giving is God's giving; all aspects of their being uphold God's representation on earth.

Knowledge of The Names (*asma'*)

The *khalifutallah* requires knowledge of all manifestable Names of God. This was the position of Prophet Adam when God declared him as a *khalifa*:

$$\text{وَإِذْ قَالَ رَبُّكَ لِلْمَلَائِكَةِ إِنِّي جَاعِلٌ فِي الْأَرْضِ خَلِيفَةً قَالُوا أَتَجْعَلُ فِيهَا مَنْ يُفْسِدُ فِيهَا وَيَسْفِكُ الدِّمَاءَ وَنَحْنُ نُسَبِّحُ بِحَمْدِكَ وَنُقَدِّسُ لَكَ قَالَ إِنِّي أَعْلَمُ مَا لَا تَعْلَمُونَ}$$

When your Lord said to the angels, 'Indeed I am going to set a viceroy on the earth', they said, 'Will You set in it someone who will cause corruption in it and shed blood, while we celebrate Your praise and proclaim Your sanctity?' He said, 'Indeed I know what you do not know.' (2:30)

In this verse, the word *khalifa* is not used in the collective sense. It refers to God placing one representative on the earth. When the angels objected, God showed them the special quality of knowledge that Prophet Adam possessed. This proved to be the tipping point in their perception of him.

The knowledge granted to Prophet Adam was manifested through the '*Names*' that God taught him. The angels argued that a *khalifa* of God had to be someone who did *taqdees* (praise) and *tasbih* (glorification). They only knew enough to be able to compare his position to their own. However, the *khalifa* needed to exceed their position, therefore, God's reply was to teach Prophet Adam the Names and show the angels a higher meaning of *taqdees* and *tasbih*, which they did not possess.

$$\text{وَعَلَّمَ آدَمَ الْأَسْمَاءَ كُلَّهَا ثُمَّ عَرَضَهُمْ عَلَى الْمَلَائِكَةِ فَقَالَ أَنْبِئُونِي بِأَسْمَاءِ هَؤُلَاءِ إِنْ كُنْتُمْ صَادِقِينَ}$$

قَالُوا سُبْحَانَكَ لَا عِلْمَ لَنَا إِلَّا مَا عَلَّمْتَنَا ۖ إِنَّكَ أَنتَ الْعَلِيمُ الْحَكِيمُ ۞

قَالَ يَا آدَمُ أَنبِئْهُم بِأَسْمَائِهِمْ ۖ فَلَمَّا أَنبَأَهُم بِأَسْمَائِهِمْ قَالَ أَلَمْ أَقُل لَّكُمْ إِنِّي أَعْلَمُ غَيْبَ السَّمَاوَاتِ وَالْأَرْضِ وَأَعْلَمُ مَا تُبْدُونَ وَمَا كُنتُمْ تَكْتُمُونَ ۞

And He taught Adam the Names, all of them; then presented them to the angels and said, 'Tell me the names of these, if you are truthful.' They said, 'Immaculate are You! We have no knowledge except what You have taught us. Indeed, You are the all-Knowing, the all-Wise.' He said, 'O Adam, inform them of their names,' and when he had informed them of their names, He said, 'Did I not tell you that I know the Unseen of the heavens and the earth and that I know whatever you disclose and whatever you conceal?' (2:31-33)

To understand the position of Prophet Adam as *khalifutallah*, which is the same position held by Imam Mahdi today, we need to analyse what these Names (*asma'*), mentioned in the Qur'anic verses, mean.

When we use or assign an *ism* (singular of *asma'*), we are in fact signalling to something. For example, if I refer to Hussain or Ahmad, it is a sign that I am alluding to someone outside or external to myself and that specific name points to a specific person. Therefore, a name is a pointer or a sign. This sign might also allude to a concept, for example, the label "hate" alludes to a concept of emotion.

Most Qur'anic exegetes have taken the view that God taught Prophet Adam the names of *everything*. This includes all concepts and all things external to himself. A tradition from Imam al Sadiq confirms the idea that "the Names" refer to the names of all things.[14] The implication here is that God taught Adam language. This is because language is the system which involves signs referring to effects. This interpretation is true in a sense because by these words we can communicate, speak our mind, and transfer our experiences.

However, words also allude to concepts that can in turn serve as names for realities. This aspect might be included in the meaning of the names. When the Qur'anic verse states *"And He taught Adam all the Names,"* it suggests that the knowledge was more encompassing than simply language. In this case, the Names have a more holistic and complete meaning. They become those means by which we gain knowledge, science, analysis and deliberation; it is through these concepts that we can investigate and discover reality. In the process of developing concepts to refer to realities, we learn how to change, modify and improve the surrounding reality and its perceptions. All our scientific advancements come from this God-given potential. Similarly, the realities which are outside the material world—the universe, human beings, feelings, angels, whatever exists in creation, could also signal to something else and thus be names for something beyond them. All these realities are Names and manifestations of God, and as such, these form an essential element of what was taught to Prophet Adam.

In the following verse, God commands Prophet Adam to display knowledge of *"their Names"*. Here a possessive pronoun is used instead of the definite article "the".

قَالَ يَٰٓـَٔادَمُ أَنۢبِئۡهُم بِأَسۡمَآئِهِمۡۖ فَلَمَّآ أَنۢبَأَهُم بِأَسۡمَآئِهِمۡ قَالَ أَلَمۡ أَقُل لَّكُمۡ إِنِّيٓ أَعۡلَمُ غَيۡبَ ٱلسَّمَٰوَٰتِ وَٱلۡأَرۡضِ وَأَعۡلَمُ مَا تُبۡدُونَ وَمَا كُنتُمۡ تَكۡتُمُونَ ۝

He said: O Adam! Inform them of **their Names**. Then when he had informed them of **their Names**, He said: Did I not say to you that I surely know what is *ghaib* in the heavens and the earth and (that) I know what you manifest and what you hide? (2:33)

The angels had no knowledge of *"their Names"* which is why they could not take the position of *khalifatullah*. They acknowledged immediately that this knowledge was beyond their capability. The use of the possessive pronoun *"their"* in this verse led to much debate among Qur'anic exegetes regarding *who* these names belonged to. Perhaps the most plausible understanding is that this knowledge referred to a realm in which everything has life and through which everything is created.

The angels did not know how they were created, yet Prophet Adam knew how they, as well as other creations, were brought to being. More importantly, he knew what Name and manifestation of God brought forth each creation and how were they connected to Him. This verse testifies to the ultimate knowledge in a created being: Prophet Adam—not the angels—possessed the Names of God that are the source of creation.

To explain this further we must realise that knowledge has degrees. For our own understanding, we may know names, in terms of language and concepts, as we are all children of Prophet Adam. We certainly have the potential to reach the level of Prophet Adam, but it requires immense purity. This is why even though these levels of knowledge exist within our potential, they cannot be retrieved.

Our hope is that when we are forgiven and go to paradise where purity is restored to our hearts, then we can witness and understand for ourselves the beautiful world awaiting us. Human beings usually end up wasting their potential in this world whilst a beautiful existence awaits them where they can reach the levels required to recognise the special Names and how they work, and experience fully the workings of God's magnificence in creation. This is the true position of *khalifatullah*.

Prophet Adam's knowledge included the understanding of all realms of creation; both the witnessed and the unseen of God's creation. This is why a collective potential is exhibited in us and is the driver for technological and scientific advancement in this world. However, the understanding of the true depth of God's creation, in this world and beyond, cannot be unlocked by us because we have not been given this responsibility of *khalifatullah* and we lack the purity to access that level.

Even among ordinary individuals, we see varying degrees of knowledge, which is why we treat this aspect of understanding and progression as being collective and deductive, in contrast to what the chosen representatives of God possess.

In what follows, a few aspects of responsibilities and qualities of the *khalifatullah* are elaborated, and the number of the *khulafa* after the Prophet will be discussed.

The Warner and The Guide

$$\text{وَيَقُولُ الَّذِينَ كَفَرُوا لَوْلَا أُنزِلَ عَلَيْهِ آيَةٌ مِّن رَّبِّهِ ۗ إِنَّمَا أَنتَ مُنذِرٌ ۖ وَلِكُلِّ قَوْمٍ هَادٍ}$$

The faithless say, 'Why has not some sign been sent down to him from his Lord?' You are only a warner, and there is a guide for every people. (13:7)

This verse has been discussed extensively by Qur'anic exegetes, especially those who were not pressured by the urgency of the political environment of the time. In the verse, God answers the constant demand from the disbelievers for the Prophet to perform a miracle. The Arabic word *ayah* has different meanings, but in the context of this verse, it means a miracle. It should be noted that no prophet had control over manifesting miracles. It is God who decides when to send a miracle and what form the miracle is to be. The Qur'an treats miracles as subordinate to the moral and spiritual evidence demonstrated by the prophets. In this verse, God replies to the disbelievers by instructing the Prophet to inform them that he is only a warner and that there is a guide for every nation (*qawm*).

In Arabic the word *qawm* has different meanings; it could refer to different people, nations or tribes and at different ages and times. Here the term means that for every instance in time, there is a guide for the people. So, while nations include many different communities, rationally *qawm* here implies that in every instance of *time* there should be at least one guide. But who are these guides?

Imam Ali is reported to have said that

> No verse of the Qur'an was ever revealed unless I knew where it was revealed. Whether it was revealed on a plain, on a mountain or while the Prophet was on a camel back or in his house. I also know about whom it was revealed and about what it was revealed.[15]

He was then asked, "What was revealed about you?" Imam Ali replied,

> Had you not asked I would not have informed you. This verse was revealed about me: 'You are only a warner, and there is a guide for every people'. The Prophet is the Warner, and I am the Guide to what he brought.[16]

This means that Imam Ali was the guide after the Prophet. There are also many traditions from the Messenger of God attesting to this fact such as the one: "*I am the Warner and Ali is the Guide.*"

In *al Durr al Manthour*, al Suyuti, the highly respected scholar from Egypt, reports that

> When the verse, "You are only a warner, and there is a guide for every people" was revealed, the Prophet put his hand on his chest and said, "I am the warner," and pointed to Ali's shoulder and said, "You are the guide. O Ali it is by you that the guided ones are guided after me."[17]

A similar tradition is reported by al Hakim al Nayshaburi in *Mustadrak al Sahihain*.[18] There, he cites many traditions stating that the Prophet is the Warner and Ali is the Guide with specially-inspired knowledge (*hujjah*). No companion or scholar can claim this prominent position.

Also, Thalabi in his *tafsir* relates on the authority of Ibn Abbas that when the verse "*And for every people there is a guide,*" was revealed, the Holy Prophet said, "*I am the Warner and Ali is the Guide. O Ali, through you, those who are guided will receive true guidance.*"[19]

Although the Prophet was mentioned in this verse as a warner, the title "warner" referring to the Prophet does not exclude the meaning of "guide" for him. The Prophet was a guide *and* a warner.

A narration from Imam Jafar al Sadiq explains that a warner is someone who guides with a revelation and a guide is someone who guides, but not necessarily with a revelation. The prophets of the Israelites who came after Prophet Musa were guides but they were not warners. This is because although they were prophets, they were guiding people to the scripture of Prophet Musa.

Imam al Baqir also said that "*the warner*" [in the verse] refers to the Holy Prophet and "*the guide*" refers to Imam Ali; then he added, "*the authority to guide continues among us.*"[20] That means the verse also points to the continued existence of a "guide" for every generation culminating to al Mahdi al Qa'im in our time.[21] The Holy Prophet is a warner for all people in all times, and the Imams from his progeny are guides for the people of every age.

Thus, although the hadith mentioned Imam Ali as the Guide, this verse cannot be restricted to him since it is general when referencing time. Kulayni reports from Imam al Sadiq that, "*The Imam of each generation is the guide for that generation.*"[22] Therefore, the Prophet mentioning Imam Ali was to demonstrate the instance of who the guide was to be immediately after him. Due to the spiritual association and in keeping with the meaning of the verse, it naturally extends to all Imams until Imam Mahdi.

The Imams after the Prophet are guides leading people to the Scripture of Prophet Muhammad, the Qur'an, and to his *sunnah*. They interpret them verbally and practically and are their preservers. However, they are not warners in the Qur'anic sense of the word. A relevant hadith from the Prophet states that: "*Scholars (ulama) of my ummah are above or better than the Prophets of Banu Israel.*"23

By scholars, the Prophet is not referring to an accomplished seeker of knowledge. Here the term scholars or *ulema* is used in its real sense, referring to those who carry true knowledge. They are the only ones that can be considered above the prophets of the Israelites because not only was their role very similar, but they also inherited the knowledge of Prophet Muhammad. The prophets of the Israelites guided people to the true meaning of Torah while the Imams after the Prophet guide to the true meaning of the Qur'an.

The Concept of Imam in the Qur'an

The Qur'an talks about several individuals whom God has appointed as Imams. The most significant is Prophet Ibrahim, who passed through numerous trials and qualifiers before God selected him as an Imam over mankind. At this point, he was already a prophet and a messenger.

وَإِذِ ابْتَلَىٰ إِبْرَاهِيمَ رَبُّهُ بِكَلِمَاتٍ فَأَتَمَّهُنَّ قَالَ إِنِّي جَاعِلُكَ لِلنَّاسِ إِمَامًا قَالَ وَمِن ذُرِّيَّتِي قَالَ لَا يَنَالُ عَهْدِي الظَّالِمِينَ ۞

When his Lord tested Ibrahim with certain words and he fulfilled them, He said, 'I am making you an Imam of mankind.' Said he, 'And from among my descendants?' He said, 'My pledge does not extend to the unjust.' (2:124)

The verse appointing Prophet Ibrahim as an Imam clearly shows that his mandate of Imamate was an expansion that extended to **all of humanity** rather than a particular region or people.

The verse links this larger mandate of Prophet Ibrahim with the passing of certain tests. The Qur'an resonates with the exceptional actions of Prophet Ibrahim: standing alone, yet unwavering, against his people for the Truth, boldly challenging the King of the time, being thrown into the fire, separation from his family, building the Kaaba, and sacrificing his son, to name a few. This sets a firm benchmark of absolute certainty, determination, unconditional patience and forbearance in the face of extreme trial and tribulation, to be the hallmarks of an Imam.

Prior to this, the Qur'an testifies to the deep knowledge of the realms and realities that were granted to Prophet Ibrahim by which he achieved this certainty:

وَكَذَٰلِكَ نُرِي إِبْرَاهِيمَ مَلَكُوتَ السَّمَاوَاتِ وَالْأَرْضِ وَلِيَكُونَ مِنَ الْمُوقِنِينَ ۞

Thus did We show Ibrahim the dominions of the heavens and the earth, that he might be of those who possess certitude. (6:75)

And it was this divine knowledge that made him a resolute Witness:

قَالَ بَل رَّبُّكُمْ رَبُّ السَّمَاوَاتِ وَالْأَرْضِ الَّذِي فَطَرَهُنَّ وَأَنَا عَلَىٰ ذَٰلِكُم مِّنَ الشَّاهِدِينَ ۞

He said, 'Indeed, your Lord is the Lord of the heavens and the earth, who originated them, and I affirm that. (21:56)

The last part of Surah al Baqarah verse 24 speaks of Prophet Ibrahim's prayer for his progeny to also be granted the same status of Imamah, which God affirms that a select group from his progeny will carry this divine mandate, with a caveat that it would not reach all of them—not the "unjust".

This caveat necessitates that anyone chosen by God as an Imam must first be pure from all sins, mistakes and ignorance, as the term "unjust" denotes, otherwise they will be unable to receive guidance from God. Any deviation from the guidance would clearly negate the basis of that guidance in the first place.

Therefore, *ismah* (purity) is a necessary pre-requisite for both Prophethood and *Imamah*. Consequently, it could only be for those from among Prophet Ibrahim's progeny who would be pure, as God's reply in 2:124 confirms, in addition to other verses re-emphasising the principles of divinely-appointed succession.

From the example of Prophet Ibrahim, we see that the qualities of an Imam are that he guides mankind, he has knowledge and certainty, and he is pure, not unjust. The central binding quality of all Imams, however, is their extreme patience. They require complete fortitude in *whatever* God decrees. This is a level that ordinary people cannot claim to possess. Absolute patience means not following personal desires, forbearance in the face of difficulties and calamities, absolute patience in matters that are seemingly confusing and beyond comprehension and persevering in obedience to God; it is an absolute submission to God.

The following is God's description of some of the Prophets from the Israelites, who were also accorded the status of Imam, based on God's promise to Prophet Ibrahim:

وَجَعَلْنَا مِنْهُمْ أَئِمَّةً يَهْدُونَ بِأَمْرِنَا لَمَّا صَبَرُوا ۖ وَكَانُوا بِآيَاتِنَا يُوقِنُونَ ۞

When they had been patient and had conviction in Our signs,
We appointed amongst them imams to guide [the people] by Our command. (32:24)

While this specific verse is about Prophet Ibrahim, Prophet Ishaq and Prophet Yaqub, it lays down the principles for God's chosen representatives. Of course, this patience is driven by unwavering certainty as the verse also mentions.

Imamate can also include non-Prophets from the progeny of Prophet Ibrahim, who are specially chosen through a process of *istifa*.[24] These non-prophetic Imams serve as guides, guardians and interpreters of the prophetic legacy.

The following Qur'anic verse defines the larger group of prophets and Imams, who were the selected recipients of this divine choice *(istifa)*:

$$\text{إِنَّ اللَّهَ اصْطَفَىٰ آدَمَ وَنُوحًا وَآلَ إِبْرَاهِيمَ وَآلَ عِمْرَانَ عَلَى الْعَالَمِينَ ۞}$$

Indeed, God chose Adam and Noah, and the progeny of Abraham and the progeny of Imran above all the nations; (3:33)

The Qur'an reiterates and explains the significance of this 'preference over all his creatures' and the mandate of Imamate given to Prophet Ibrahim's progeny, in other verses Qur'an. For example:

$$\text{أَمْ يَحْسُدُونَ النَّاسَ عَلَىٰ مَا آتَاهُمُ اللَّهُ مِن فَضْلِهِ ۖ فَقَدْ آتَيْنَا آلَ إِبْرَاهِيمَ الْكِتَابَ وَالْحِكْمَةَ وَآتَيْنَاهُم مُّلْكًا عَظِيمًا ۞}$$

Do they envy those people for what Allah has given them out of His bounty? We have certainly given the progeny of Abraham the Book and wisdom, and We have given them a great sovereignty. (4:54)

$$\text{وَوَهَبْنَا لَهُ إِسْحَاقَ وَيَعْقُوبَ وَجَعَلْنَا فِي ذُرِّيَّتِهِ النُّبُوَّةَ وَالْكِتَابَ وَآتَيْنَاهُ أَجْرَهُ فِي الدُّنْيَا ۖ وَإِنَّهُ فِي الْآخِرَةِ لَمِنَ الصَّالِحِينَ ۞}$$

And We gave him Isaac and Jacob, and **We ordained among his descendants prophethood and the Book**, and We gave him his reward in this world, and in the Hereafter he will indeed be among the Righteous. (29:27)

The phrases *'kitab wal hikmah'* meaning 'the Book and Wisdom' and *'nabuwata wal kitab'* meaning 'Prophethood and the Book' in the above verses includes the aspects of revelation through Prophets and also its true interpretation and legacy through non-Prophetic Imams, remaining within the progeny of Prophet Ibrahim.

Therefore, an ordinary believer can never be an Imam, as their faith can be shaken when tested in their journey of spiritual growth. They may develop strong faith but cannot reach the highest level of certainty. Moreover, Imams are divinely chosen (*istafah*); they maintain a constant connection with God and are Divinely-inspired towards good. The following verse elaborates further on the characteristics of an Imam when speaking about Prophet Ibrahim, Prophet Ishaq and Prophet Yaqub:

وَجَعَلْنَاهُمْ أَئِمَّةً يَهْدُونَ بِأَمْرِنَا وَأَوْحَيْنَا إِلَيْهِمْ فِعْلَ الْخَيْرَاتِ وَإِقَامَ الصَّلَاةِ وَإِيتَاءَ الزَّكَاةِ وَكَانُوا لَنَا عَابِدِينَ ۞

We made them imams, guiding by Our command, and We revealed to them [concerning] the performance of good deeds, the maintenance of prayers, and the giving of zakat, and they used to worship Us. (21:73)

This verse defines clearly what an Imam is. They are connected to a divine realm of continuous guidance. Virtue and good actions gush forth from them. There is no conflict or contradiction between their speech and their actions.

It is also worth reflecting that despite being appointed an Imam for mankind, no narration suggests that Prophet Ibrahim had any form of government or many people following him. Yet his presence, over 4000 years ago, so deeply impacted human trajectory that his call continues to echo in our lives. He is a prime example of the deep influence a chosen Imam of God has on the world, despite not being widely known or accessible. So distinguished in God's esteem was Prophet Ibrahim, that the Qur'an uses the term *ummah* for his person alone.

$$\text{إِنَّ إِبْرَاهِيمَ كَانَ أُمَّةً قَانِتًا لِلَّهِ حَنِيفًا وَلَمْ يَكُ مِنَ الْمُشْرِكِينَ ۞}$$
$$\text{شَاكِرًا لِأَنْعُمِهِ اجْتَبَاهُ وَهَدَاهُ إِلَىٰ صِرَاطٍ مُّسْتَقِيمٍ ۞}$$

Indeed Abraham was a nation [all by himself], obedient to Allah, a Hanif, and he was not a polytheist. Grateful [as he was] for His blessings, He chose him and guided him to a straight path. (16:120 121)

Prophet Muhammad, as a descendant of Prophet Ibrahim, is the great personage Prophet Ibrahim and Prophet Ismail specifically prayed for poignantly after raising the walls of the Ka'ba. This was done after humbly requesting for continued submission and for the continuity of true servants of God within their progeny.

$$\text{رَبَّنَا وَاجْعَلْنَا مُسْلِمَيْنِ لَكَ وَمِن ذُرِّيَّتِنَا أُمَّةً مُّسْلِمَةً لَّكَ وَأَرِنَا مَنَاسِكَنَا وَتُبْ عَلَيْنَا إِنَّكَ أَنتَ التَّوَّابُ الرَّحِيمُ ۞}$$

$$\text{رَبَّنَا وَابْعَثْ فِيهِمْ رَسُولًا مِّنْهُمْ يَتْلُو عَلَيْهِمْ آيَاتِكَ وَيُعَلِّمُهُمُ الْكِتَابَ وَالْحِكْمَةَ وَيُزَكِّيهِمْ إِنَّكَ أَنتَ الْعَزِيزُ الْحَكِيمُ ۞}$$

'Our Lord, make us submissive to You, and [raise] from our progeny a nation submissive to You, and show us our rites [of worship], and turn to us clemently. Indeed, You are the All-Clement, the All-Merciful.'
'Our Lord, raise amongst them an apostle from among them, who will recite to them Your signs and teach them the Book and wisdom and purify them. Indeed, You are the All-Mighty, the All-Wise.' (2:128-129)

A prophet's prayer always manifests the truth and thus, the first prayer proves that there were always men and women from Prophet Ibrahim's and Prophet Ismail's progeny who carried the light of true faith in the entire period leading up to Prophet Muhammad.

The prayer of Prophet Ibrahim for a *"Messenger among them"* was not his personal desire but rather a testament to his striving and the striving of prophets and imams before and after him, towards God's Will. It indicates their role and effort in preparing and paving the way for the Final Messenger and the Mercy to the Worlds that Prophet Muhammad embodied.

This is why the *Imamate* of Prophet Ibrahim has become an everlasting example and a fountainhead for all Imamate that followed within his progeny. It is also the reason why *Durood Ibrahimi* is such an integral part of Islamic faith:

اللَّهُمَّ صَلِّ عَلَىٰ مُحَمَّدٍ وَعَلَىٰ آلِ مُحَمَّدٍ
كَمَا صَلَّيْتَ عَلَىٰ إِبْرَاهِيمَ وَعَلَىٰ آلِ إِبْرَاهِيمَ إِنَّكَ حَمِيدٌ مَجِيدٌ

O God, bestow Your favour on Muhammad and on the family of Muhammad as You have bestowed Your favour on Ibrahim and on the family of Ibrahim, You are Praiseworthy, Most Glorious.

This prayer and the shorter *salawat* we send on Prophet Muhammad and his progeny are so essential that no obligatory prayer is complete without the latter. In reality, it forms a required and necessary connection whilst simultaneously testifying to our own belief as Muslims in this divinely-granted status and its everlasting continuity.

So elevated is the merit of *salawat* that the Qur'an states:

إِنَّ اللَّهَ وَمَلَائِكَتَهُ يُصَلُّونَ عَلَى النَّبِيِّ يَا أَيُّهَا الَّذِينَ آمَنُوا صَلُّوا عَلَيْهِ وَسَلِّمُوا تَسْلِيمًا ۞

Indeed, God and His angels bless the Prophet; O you who have faith! Invoke blessings on him and invoke Peace upon him in a worthy manner. (33:56)

The verse clearly expresses that *salawat* is a perpetual and ceaseless act of God and His Angels. It is not something that was done in the past that we are commanded to emulate but an act that continues in all realms and across all times of creation perpetually. By reciting it we become part of a divine act and are thus connected to higher realms of existence, awareness, and testimony to the obedience of the ones chosen by God.

The Concept of the *Hujjah* (Proof)

The concept of the *hujjah* (proof) is closely linked to the previous principles and terminologies discussed. The term *hujjah* is used to describe the Imam's presence that radiates the testimony of the oneness of God, points towards His justice and mercy and validates His reason for the creation of humans and their elevation above any other of His Creation.

The *hujjah's* presence validates the chosen system of guidance that is in effect and thus, he becomes a proof against the feeble excuses of evil-doers. A *hujjah* manifests this proof, standing or sitting, speaking or silent and whether accessible or inaccessible.

In a report from Kumayl, which will be discussed shortly, Imam Ali explains why a guide is needed for every era:. "*So that the proofs of God and His clear evidence are not invalidated.*" In fact, the existence of the *hujjah* at every time is an article of faith received from the Ahlul Bayt, as a *hadith* reported in *al Kafi* states from Abu Abdillah, "*If no one remains on the earth except two people one of them will be the hujjah.*" And he added, "*The last one who dies is the Imam so that no one can provide an argument against God that He left him without a proof.*"[25]

Another similar hadith says: "*If people [on the earth] are only two, one of them would be the Imam.*"[26]

The core idea here is that there is always an individual on the earth with the special knowledge that has been bestowed on him by God. In a proper sense, the difference between the Shia and Sunni schools is not really about who should have been the political caliph after the Prophet. Even if that is the case, it is history and now out of context. It is ridiculous for us to argue after 1400 years whether Abu Bakr should have been the first political caliph or Imam Ali. Rather, central to Shia theology and understanding of how God guides creation is the belief that there is always someone on the earth with that knowledge which was bestowed by God to the Prophet. This is the only person who should be absolutely obeyed if guidance is to be achieved.

The Continuity of *Hujjah*: Imam Ali's Walk with Kumayl:

There is a famous hadith narrated from Imam Ali reported in many different books of both Shia and Sunni scholars, including Sheikh Saduq and Imam Ghazali. Ghazali has dedicated a long discussion to this hadith and its contents in his book *Ihiya'u 'Ulum al Dīn*.

The hadith is a conversation between Imam Ali and his dedicated disciple, Kumayl ibn Ziyad as it is reported in *Nahjul Balagha* by Sharif al Razi. Only the relevant parts of this conversation will be discussed here. The background to this conversation, according to Kumayl, was that one night he found Imam Ali in a melancholic state, frustrated by what was transpiring around him after the demise of the Prophet. He invited Kumayl to take a walk with him and as they moved outside the city, the Imam started speaking to him in a sorrowful tone.

> O Kumail, knowledge is better than wealth; knowledge protects you while you protect wealth. Wealth diminishes with spending while knowledge swells with spreading.

Knowledge brings peace and tranquillity to the mind and advances both the individual and society, whereas wealth becomes the cause of theft, strife and war. Then he pointed to his chest and said: "Here rests accumulated knowledge; I wish I could find someone to carry it."[27]

Here one may wonder why Kumayl, a close disciple of the Imam, could not have acquired the knowledge that the Imam was referring to. The fact that he could not, shows that closeness or remoteness to the Imam is not a criterion for receiving this knowledge. It requires a specific capacity and aptitude. In the narration, Imam Ali goes on to explain that some people may have the capacity to receive knowledge but indulge in the pleasures of the world, whilst others are committed to the faith but do not have the capacity for this knowledge. "*This is how knowledge dies with the death of those who carry it,*" he concludes.

Then he ends with a firm statement. "*Yet, by God, the earth is never going to be without the one who rises for God with proof, (be he) either known and manifest or hidden and fearful. So that the proof of God and His clear evidence is not invalidated.*"

This hadith indicates that the presence of a person who exists as the inheritor of the prophetic knowledge at all times is guaranteed by God. Such people are not great in number, but they are crucial for continuity of the prophetic knowledge on earth. They have the capacity to receive that knowledge and to preserve it. If there was not someone like Ali ibn Abi Talib with the capacity to receive from the Prophet, the knowledge of the Prophet would have departed from the earth when he died. Similarly, Imam Hasan inherited this knowledge from his father and Imam Hussein from him. In this way, the Imams are the inheritors of all the previous prophets in a continuing chain of guidance for humanity. As we say in the salutations to Imam Husayn:

> Peace be upon you, O inheritor of Adam, the choice of God.
> Peace be upon you, O inheritor of Nuh, the prophet of God.

Peace be upon you, O inheritor of Ibrahim, the intimate friend of God. Peace be upon you, O inheritor of Musa, the one spoken to by God. Peace be upon you, O inheritor of Isa, the spirit of God. Peace be upon you, O inheritor of Muhammad, the most beloved by God.[28]

Accessibility to the *Hujjah* (Proof)

Imam Mahdi is commonly known as *Hujjat ibn Hasan* or the *Hujjah*. This is one of his most significant titles. However, one may justifiably question how beneficial this preserved knowledge is if it cannot be transferred to ordinary people. The answer requires us to broaden our view and understand that while this knowledge cannot be transferred in full to ordinary people, it is available even when it is not accessible. The issue is not about individuals being able to access it or not, it is about the human race.

Our societies have deprived us—individually and collectively—of access to the possessors of this knowledge throughout the ages. In the early Islamic period, the Imams could not be reached by all those who wished to benefit from their knowledge. They were imprisoned, placed under house arrest, or forced to remote regions where access was not easily transmitted, or even possible, for everyone. Therefore, it was never the Imams who placed barriers to their knowledge, but political and social conditions that hindered contact. This behaviour has been repeated throughout time with many of the prophets of God and the authorities of their times.

We must remind ourselves that God has taken it as a duty upon Himself to place these special representatives on the earth. It is our responsibility to remove any barriers so that everyone who seeks to can have access to them. Perhaps the better question we should ask ourselves is whether we are compatible recipients for whatever portion of that knowledge is transferable were it to be made accessible to us?

To further explore this issue, we need to remind ourselves that

God sent many Books, but people continuously rejected them. Although hundreds of prophets were killed by the dissidents, God kept sending them. He carries out His plan of guidance whether people accept it or not. The absence of the Imam is not because God does not want him to guide mankind, but because we as a human race are heedless and not in the frame of mind to accept him.

One should ponder on the fate of the Imams preceding Imam Mahdi; they were rejected, imprisoned, poisoned, and killed by the very people they were sent to guide. Yet they remained the carriers of knowledge and God did not leave the earth empty of them. God has always had a *hujjah* present in all times but how people treated them is a different matter. God always sent prophets; how people received them differed. Given that Imam Mahdi is the Final Proof from God, this is an important point to consider.

Guidance is God's responsibility as the verse states,

$$\text{إِنَّ عَلَيْنَا لَلْهُدَىٰ}$$

Indeed, guidance rests with Us. (92:12)

God always does what He has made incumbent upon Himself. It is we who need to ponder about our treatment of His guidance. We argue that the Imam is absent and question the philosophy of a hidden existence and how it translates into guidance for us. What we must understand is that the philosophy of his presence is not based on us finding a way to communicate with him, it is founded on the principle that if he were not present on Earth with the divine knowledge and connection granted to him, the human race would reach the end of its purpose and the Day of Judgment would arrive.

This raises a second question: How can human existence be predicated on one or even a handful of individuals? To understand this, we must properly examine the purpose of human existence on this earth according to the Qur'an and *hadith*.

Firstly, the *hujjah* may be manifest and known, as many of the prophets were, or he may be unknown. Imam Ali himself was unknown to most people. Sometimes these select persons were fearful for their lives, and they needed to be unknown or at least, not popularly seen and heard. Most of the Imams had to contend with living in such situations, and Imam Mahdi is facing a similar circumstance.

The *hadith* of Imam Ali quoted earlier states, "*And how many are they and where do they dwell; by God, their number is few but their value with God is great. Through them, God preserves His proofs and His clear evidence until they entrust it to their counterparts and sow it in the hearts of their likes.*"[29]

Here Imam Ali emphasises that the number of people with inspired knowledge from God is very limited. The inspiration entrusted to them is sown in their spiritual successors. It is not knowledge they learn from books or leave behind in writings so that their successor can read and follow it. It goes from heart to heart, just like the knowledge of the Prophet that went from his heart to the heart of Imam Ali who became his spiritual successor. The quality of their knowledge and its method of acquisition is very different from our knowledge and the means we use to obtain it.

"*They accompany this world with bodies the souls of which cling to the higher realm. These are the viceroys of God in His Earth and the callers to His faith.*"[30] This hadith highlights the two reasons why the *hujjah* must be present; he is the viceroy of God on this earth and the caller to His faith.

The reality is that if we relied solely on the Qur'an and standard scholars to settle our disputes, we would argue against each other in vain without being sure who is right or wrong. Without the Imam, the greatest *hujjah*—the Qur'an—is weakened because nobody can know its true interpretation with certainty.

Imam Jafar al Sadiq met a man who had travelled from Damascus to debate with him.[31] The Imam asked him on what principle he would debate and when he replied that he would use the Qur'an as a basis, the Imam questioned if the Qur'an alone could remove differences, then why had he come to debate? This incident illustrates that although the Qur'an is the greatest *hujjah*, it is not sufficient without a guide. It requires a speaking *hujjah* who can interpret it; who makes the *hujjah* of the Qur'an complete.

The Qur'an can be interpreted or misinterpreted in many different ways. A modern example can be seen in how ISIS/Daesh have rigidly interpreted the Qur'an to justify their brutality and abhorrent misconduct. On the other side of the spectrum, the Qur'an is loosely interpreted by so-called moderate Muslims who adapt the verses to "modern standards of human life" by denying all its precepts. Shias, Sunnis, Mu'taziles, Asharites and all denominations of Muslims have understood the Qur'an in different ways, and the varying interpretations show that the Qur'an cannot be enough on its own. This Holy Book contains immensely deep and diverse injunctions for mankind and without a guide, its meanings can be easily misunderstood.

The Qur'an may guide us individually, but it cannot guide us as a community on its own. Communities disagree with one another over its interpretation – each sect reciting and understanding the Qur'an according to its own school of thought. Over centuries, the Qur'an has not been able to remove the differences between the Shia and the Sunni, the Ash'ari and the Mu'tazili, the Sufi and the Salafi, the Hanfi and the Hanbali, and so on. It cannot unite opinions unless there is a *hujjah* present to settle its interpretation. The Qur'an itself states that the Prophet is the arbitrator of differences:

يَا أَيُّهَا الَّذِينَ آمَنُوا أَطِيعُوا اللَّهَ وَأَطِيعُوا الرَّسُولَ وَأُولِي الْأَمْرِ مِنكُمْ فَإِن تَنَازَعْتُمْ فِي شَيْءٍ فَرُدُّوهُ إِلَى اللَّهِ وَالرَّسُولِ إِن كُنتُمْ تُؤْمِنُونَ بِاللَّهِ وَالْيَوْمِ الْآخِرِ ۚ ذَٰلِكَ خَيْرٌ وَأَحْسَنُ تَأْوِيلًا ۞

O you who have faith! Obey God and obey the Apostle and those vested with authority among you. And if you dispute concerning anything, refer it to God and the Apostle, if you have faith in God and the Last Day. That is better and more favourable in outcome. (4:59)

The Prophet's true successors continue this arbitration after him. In fact, *Imamah* is an institution for removing differences. In her awe-inspiring sermon, the noble Lady Fatima states that: "*God has legislated obeying us* [Ahlul Bayt] *for the management of the nation, and our leadership as a safeguard from disunity. It is a security from differences, if we obey.*"[32]

Having said that, it may be argued that the above does not apply to Imam Mahdi since he is not present and cannot arbitrate even if we wanted to seek it. The counter-question is can he or God be faulted or is it the human community in general that is not ready to receive him, with some even looking to kill him? The *hujjah* is necessary as a part of the process of channelling general guidance (*hidayatullah*) from God to human beings; he must be present and kept safe for this reason.

There is an anecdotal perception that if a pious *alim* makes a mistake, the Imam communicates with him to correct him and that this kind of guidance is a purpose of the *hujjah*. However, this is not the guidance referred to in the narrations confirming the necessity of his presence on the earth. The necessity is by decree of the just and merciful system that God has created for mankind. The benefits may not necessarily be visible, but they do exist.

Without *hujjah* the whole system of guidance is lacking. It is reported from Imam al Reza that: "*The proof of God over His creation cannot be established except through an Imam so that He is known.*"[33] We can know God through the Qur'an, but we still need someone who can extract the knowledge from it and explain Him to us.

The tradition quoted above explains that there is always an Imam as a guide so that people would not have any argument on the Day of Judgement that no guidance was available for those who sought or needed one. We can imagine that God may treat those who did not have access to that Imam leniently, especially if they were not one of those culprits who hindered Imam in his duty. Such people could be regarded as *mustazaf* (weak on the earth) because of their lack of access. There would still not be any credible argument against God for not sending an Imam. The Imam is here; the *hujjah* (proof) has always been here.

One may wonder whether it is even possible that God would allow anyone to stand before Him on Judgement Day and argue with Him regarding such an issue. Multiple verses in the Qur'an refer to people making different kinds of complaints and excuses to God. He will let people put forward their cases because He is Kind, Generous and His system of accountability is based on His Divine Justice and Mercy. In this world too, He allows us, without compulsion or force, to form our own arguments and understanding before being considered believers or disbelievers.

Similarly, on the Day of Judgement, people will be allowed to bring forth whatever defence they have concerning what hindered them from going towards God. People will present a variety of excuses and arguments, which will be heard, and witnesses will be allowed before the final judgement is made. We may view these conversations as terrifying, but it only highlights that even in His Divine Justice, God is Beneficent, Generous and Merciful towards His creation.

In a beautiful hadith, Imam al Sadiq is reported to have said, "*The entire Qur'an looks like a rebuke, but its deeper purpose is to bring people close.*"[34] When we recite the verses of the Qur'an, we can see a clear pattern of admonition. Imam al Sadiq explains however that this actually shows you the path to seeking nearness to Him, as the verse explains:

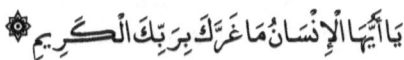

O man! What has deceived you about your generous Lord? (82:6)

If we read Qur'anic verses from this perspective, we will see that all the descriptions of the Day of Judgement point to a very gracious God who, despite being aware of everything, allows us to argue and realise the truth by ourselves.

The *hujjah* is part of the same system of divine grace and mercy that eradicates every valid argument for man to persist in disbelief.

The Twelve Successors

In the aforementioned conversation of Imam Ali with Kumail, he explained that the 'proofs' are small in number but great in their value with God. An important question which pauses itself here is how many are these 'proofs' after the Prophet?

To answer this question let us begin by an interesting anecdote from the early history of Islam involving the famous scribe and scholar of the Qur'an Abdullah Ibn Mas'ud. Masruq ibn Ajda'(d. 62 AH) reports that they were in the company of Abdullah b. Mas'ud checking their copies of Qur'an with him, when suddenly a young man asked him, "*Did our Prophet inform you how many successors would be after him?*" This question surprised Ibn Masud as he did not expect anyone to publicly ask this kind of question given the political environment and historical conflict regarding the matter. So, he replied, "*You are young and inexperienced; otherwise, you would never have asked such a question in this climate. This is an issue about which no one has asked me before."* Abdullah ibn Masud himself was a very frank and daring man, so he continued, *"Yes, our Prophet informed us that there will be twelve successors after him, the same number as the chiefs of the Children of Israel."*[35]

There is ample evidence in canonical Sunni and Shia sources of *hadith* to show that the number of *khalifa*s or successors after the Prophet is twelve. Numerous traditions report the Prophet stating at various instances that there will be twelve *khalifa*s after him. The word *khalifa* (pl. *khulafa*) in these traditions refers to them as being both *khalifatu rasulallah* (Successor to the Prophet) as well as *khalifatullah* (Vicegerent of God).

Al Bukhari, al Muslim, al Tirmidhi, Abu Dawood and Ahmad b. Hanbal have all reported—through various chains of transmissions—from Jabir b. Samurah that he heard the Prophet saying, *"Islam continues with its dignity until twelve successors are in place."*[36] or in the words of al Bukhari, *"There will be twelve princes."*[37] In other narrations, the Prophet is quoted as saying, *"This matter would not expire before twelve caliphs have come forth, all of whom are from Quraysh."*[38] or *"This Umma has twelve guardians; those who desert them would not harm them, and all of them are from Quraysh."*[39] These tradition are reported with different wordings by numerous other reporters as well.

Although these traditions have caused confusion and debate amongst the Sunni schools and some smaller branches of Shias (mainly Ismailis and Zaidis), no one has ever doubted their authenticity.

The hadith referring to *"twelve guardians from the Quraysh"* was used as an argument by Abu Bakr in the event of Saqifa. When the Ansar argued that they have to choose two successors after the Prophet, one from the Ansar and another from the Muhajiroon, Abu Bakr countered, *"Haven't you heard from the Prophet who* said, *'The Imams are from Quraysh?'*⁴⁰ The wordings used here are very similar to other narrations that state the twelve *khulafa* are from Quraysh. The tribe of Quraysh is a huge tribe with various subtribes, and we can conclude that any of them, including the Banu Hashim, was intended by the Prophet. *"This ummah has twelve guardians; those who desert them would not harm them, and all of them are from Quraysh."*⁴¹

In discussing traditions such as these, scholars like al Bukhari and Muslim have accepted that they cannot fully understand the meaning and implications of these traditions. In an attempt to count twelve *khulafa*, they count the first four *'Khulafa al Rashidoon',* they exclude Imam Hasan (though some others include him as he was the political Caliph for a short while) and then they count the 8th Umayyad Caliph, Omar bin Abdul Aziz, who ruled from 99 to 101 AH, as the fifth, while the remaining seven *khulafa* are left unaccounted for. Certainly, the likes of Yazid ibn Mu'awiyah or Abdul Malik ibn Marwan cannot be included among the successors of the Prophet. That is why some Sunni scholars have said that six of these rulers are unknown to the people, and the last one is the Mahdi.⁴²

At any rate, there is no plausible explanation from Sunni scholars who the remaining *khulafa* are, and they have conceded that the full understanding of this narration remains enigmatic within general Sunni scholarship. In his interpretation of *Sunan of al Tirmidhi*, the jurist Abu Bakr Ibn al Arabi (d. 543 AH), admits that the meaning of this narration could not be understood.⁴³ The famous Sunni scholar Jalaluddin Al Suyuti (d.911 AH) considers the awaited Mahdi from the Holy Family to be one of the twelve, but he says that we do not know who all the twelve are. He postulates that they may gradually manifest themselves over time, but one of them will be the Mahdi and he is yet to be born.⁴⁴

Interestingly, there have been some prominent Sunni scholars who have not only confirmed Imam Mahdi as being the son of

Imam Hassan al Askari but have confirmed all preceding Imams as well.

The famous Sunni mystic Shaykh Muhyuddin ibn Arabi (d. 637AH), also referred to as al Shaykh al Akbar by Sufi scholars, wrote in *Futuhat Makkiyah*:

> Know that the advent of the Mahdi is imminent, but he will not stage an uprising till the earth is not full of injustice and tyranny so that he may fill it with justice and equity. He is from the progeny of the Holy Prophet and is a descendant of Lady Fatima Zahra. His grandfather is Imam Husayn ibn Ali ibn Abi Talib, and his father is Imam al Hassan Askari ibn Ali al Naqi ibn Imam Muhammad al Taqi ibn Imam Ali al Reza ibn Imam Musa al Kazim ibn Imam Ja'far al Sadiq ibn Imam Muhammad al Baqir ibn Imam Zainul al Abideen ibn Imam Husayn ibn Imam Ali Ibn Abi Talib. His name is the same as the name of the Messenger of God. Muslims will pay him allegiance between Rukn and Maqam. He will be like the Prophet in appearance and the manners and the conduct of the Prophet will be present in him.[45]

The Twelver Shias, however, have no doubt on this matter. For them, it is very clear that the twelve *khulafa* from Quraysh are the twelve specific Imams from Ahlul Bayt, and that the Mahdi is the son of Imam Hasan al Askari.

The Twelve *Muhaddath*

The Holy Prophet is reported to have said, "*From my Ahlul Bayt there will be twelve muhaddath.*"[46]

From what we discussed so far, it is obvious that an Imam, be him a prophet or not, must have some connection and communication with the higher realm, otherwise he could not be a guide from God, guiding by His command. The question is if an Imam is not a prophet, then what type of communication does he receive from God? This is where the idea of *muhaddath* becomes relevant.

The word *muhaddath* in Arabic is from *tahdith* which is a term that appears repeatedly in the *hadith* corpus. It literally means "someone who is spoken to" and refers to one who is spoken to by the angels. Thus, the Imam is someone who communicates with the angels. This must not confuse their status with those of prophets who receive revelation through angels, because divine communication can have different levels and methods.

Al Kulayni has dedicated a chapter in *al Kafi* to clarify the meaning of *muhaddath* and its difference between a prophet (*nabi*) and a messenger (*rasul*) in terms of the types of communication that they receive from God.[47]

The concept appears in early exegetical sources too. In the commentary of the verse 22:52:

وَمَا أَرْسَلْنَا مِنْ قَبْلِكَ مِنْ رَسُولٍ وَلَا نَبِيٍّ إِلَّا إِذَا تَمَنَّىٰ أَلْقَى الشَّيْطَانُ فِي أُمْنِيَّتِهِ فَيَنْسَخُ اللَّهُ مَا يُلْقِي الشَّيْطَانُ ثُمَّ يُحْكِمُ اللَّهُ آيَاتِهِ وَاللَّهُ عَلِيمٌ حَكِيمٌ ۞

We did not send any apostle or prophet before you but that when he recited [the scripture] Satan interjected [something] in his recitation. Thereat God nullifies whatever Satan has interjected, and then God confirms His signs, and God is All-Knowing, All-Wise. (22:52)[48]

Ibn Abbas has added *muhaddath* after *rasul* (apostle) and *nabi* (prophet) in the verse as an explanation indicating that a *nabi*, a *rasul* and a *muhaddath* have almost the same status in this respect.

According to Kulayni, a *muhaddath* is someone who can hear the voice of an angel without seeing them.[49] This is distinct from a messenger (*rasul*) who hears the voice and can see the angel too.

Once Imam al Baqir was asked by his followers how the Imams receive knowledge. He replied that it was through an inscription in the heart - *naktun fi al qalb*, an inspiration in the heart - *qadhfun fi al qalb* or a striking in the ears - *naqrun fi al asma*.[50] These are experiences that cannot be fully described with words, especially for those who cannot fathom the spiritual experience. Does it come as literal thoughts? Or meanings? Or concepts? It can be difficult to discern the different types of divine communication without any experience of them.

The main aspect of this idea is that despite possessing this quality of being *muhaddath*, the Imams categorically denied that they were prophets or had prophetic experiences. This was confusing even for some of the companions of the Imams who still could not discriminate between the Imam's position and the prophetic experience of revelation. Once Imam al Baqir said that Imam Ali was a *muhaddath*. His companion, Harith bin al Mughayrah asked, "Do you, therefore, mean that he was a Prophet?" The Imam denied this and said,

> No, rather like the companion of Musa, [Khizr], or the companion of Sulayman, Asif ibn Barkhia who brought the throne of Bilqis from Yemen, or like Dhul Qarnain. Have you not heard that on the mention of Dhul Qarnain, the Prophet said that amongst you is the like of him? There is someone like Dhul Qarnain among you communicated to by God through angels but he does not see the angels.[51]

This concept of *muhaddath* appears in Sunni *hadith* literature as well. Both al Bukhari and Muslim report from the Prophet that: "*In the nations that passed before you there were people who were muhaddath, and if one such person could be found in my ummah it is Umar b. al Khattab.*"[52] Furthermore, another narration in al Bukhari says, "*In those who passed before you from the Children of Israel, there were men who were spoken to [by God] without being prophets, and if one of them exists in my ummah he should be Umar.*"[53]

The last part of the sentence is apparently an addition by the reporters. From a Sunni perspective, there could be no better candidate than Umar Ibn Khattab to have this position, as he does enjoy great reverence among them. However, neither did he claim such abilities nor did he display a high degree of that type of knowledge. Therefore, the explanation is implausible and Shias would discard it as an addition to the narration.

What is important to focus on here is that the concept of *muhaddath*—people who are spoken to without being prophets—has appeared in Sunni hadith as well. Of course, the Qur'anic verses referring to Khizr, Maryam, Dhul Qarnain and the mother of Musa are quite clear and undisputed on the matter as well.

The above hadith attributed to the Prophet denies the existence of any *muhaddath* among the Prophet's *ummah*. However, it is highly implausible that the *muhaddathun* were only from the people who existed in the lineage of other prophets and communities but not among Prophet Muhammad's *ummah*. Thus, as stated, one can only conclude that the last part of the narration is some sort of explanation added by the reporter.

The reality is that such traditions allude to concepts that are deeply difficult to explain. Thus, they have not been viewed with much significance by Sunni scholars and, therefore, have not found a place at the heart of Sunni theology. Nevertheless, the existence of these narrations ignited a series of discussions about the concept of *muhaddath* in Sunni scholarly writings which dealt with the implications of the spiritual position of *muhaddath*.

For example, al Manawi, a 10th-century Egyptian scholar and Qur'anic commentator, writes on the subject: *"Muhaddath is an inspired person on whose soul things descend from the higher realm as inspiration or unveiling, or someone whose tongue speaks the truth without intending it, or someone to whom the angels speak without being a prophet."* [54]

The idea of someone being inspired and angels speaking to them without them being a prophet definitely exists within Muslim scope of thought. The explanation from al Manawi is reminiscent of the expressions such as *naktun fi al qalb* (inscription in the heart) and *qadhfun fi al qalb* (inspiration in the heart) or *naqrun fi al asma* (striking in the ears) used by the Imams of Ahlul Bayt who have explained the concept more clearly to us.

The concurrence of twelve *muhaddath* with twelve *khulafa* in the hadith of the Prophet promotes the idea of twelve infallible Imams as the Shia believe.

Muhaddath and *Siddiq*

The Qur'an connects the concept of *muhaddath* with another title—*siddiq*—which is mentioned in verse 69 of Surah al Nisa as a position just below the position of the prophets.

وَمَنْ يُطِعِ اللَّهَ وَالرَّسُولَ فَأُولَٰئِكَ مَعَ الَّذِينَ أَنْعَمَ اللَّهُ عَلَيْهِمْ مِنَ النَّبِيِّينَ وَالصِّدِّيقِينَ وَالشُّهَدَاءِ وَالصَّالِحِينَ وَحَسُنَ أُولَٰئِكَ رَفِيقًا ۞

Whoever obeys God and the Apostle—they are with those whom God has blessed, including the prophets and the truthful (*siddiqeen*), the witnesses and the righteous, and excellent companions are they! (4:69)

The idea of people communicating with angels without having been appointed as prophets is invoked in the Qur'an. The example in the Qur'an that links the idea of *muhaddath* to *siddiq* and *siddiqah* is the outstanding one of Lady Maryam, the mother of Prophet Isa. We are told in the Qur'an that angels communicated with her at a very young age.

وَإِذْ قَالَتِ الْمَلَائِكَةُ يَا مَرْيَمُ إِنَّ اللَّهَ اصْطَفَاكِ وَطَهَّرَكِ وَاصْطَفَاكِ عَلَىٰ نِسَاءِ الْعَالَمِينَ ۞

And when the angels said, 'O Mary, God has chosen you and purified you, and He has chosen you above all the women of the world'. (3:42)

Despite this explicit verse and other similar verses about Maryam's communication with angels, it is almost unanimously held by Muslim theologians that she was not a prophetess. This necessitates the existence of an intermediate position between the rank of the prophets and the state of the normal people who are completely shut out of the realm of the angels. Therefore, the concept of *muhaddath* is not strange nor is it out of place. It is part of Qur'anic understanding.

With regards to Maryam, the Qur'an describes her as being a *siddiqah*, a woman who is truthful.

مَا الْمَسِيحُ ابْنُ مَرْيَمَ إِلَّا رَسُولٌ قَدْ خَلَتْ مِنْ قَبْلِهِ الرُّسُلُ وَأُمُّهُ صِدِّيقَةٌ ۞

The Messiah, son of Mary, is but an apostle. Certainly, [other] apostles have passed before him, and his mother was a truthful one. (5:75)

One issue that arises from the story of Maryam is that in addition to hearing angels, she later *saw* Angel Gabriel:

فَاتَّخَذَتْ مِنْ دُونِهِمْ حِجَابًا فَأَرْسَلْنَا إِلَيْهَا رُوحَنَا فَتَمَثَّلَ لَهَا بَشَرًا سَوِيًّا ۞

Thus did she seclude herself from them, whereupon We sent to her Our Spirit and he became incarnate for her as a well-proportioned human. (19:17)

This needs to be reconciled with the explanation by the Imam which says the difference between the prophet and the *muhaddath* (or *muhaddatha*) is that the prophet can *see* the angel and the *muhaddath* cannot. Either we have to conclude that the hadith cited in *al Kafi* is incomplete and lacking a full explanation or an alternative explanation needs to be found.

The conclusion is straightforward; it is sometimes possible for others, even ordinary humans, to see angels in cases where the angels only reveal matters to them which are related to their personal affairs. For example, Sarah, the wife of Prophet Ibrahim, saw the angels and conversed with them when they visited her bringing news of the birth of Prophet Ishaq, yet she is not known or mentioned in the Qur'an or traditions as a *muhaddatha*.

Even perverted people sometimes are made to see angels in the form of human beings. The people of Prophet Lut saw the angels who came to bring down the punishment on them.

Therefore, seeing angels may, at times, be possible for ordinary people too. However, merly seeing angels should be distinguished from true communication with them which comes as an inscription in the heart, an inspiration in the soul, or a striking in the ears as happens for the *muhaddath*; and this must be distinguished from revelation of the Scripture or communication with a prophet.

At any rate, as well as being a *muhaddatha*, Lady Maryam is placed in the category *siddiqeen*, 'the truthful', as mentioned in Surah Maidah, verse 75:

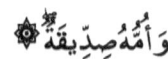

And his mother was (*siddiqah*), a truthful one... (5:75)

Siddiqah is the feminine form for *siddiq*, the plural of which is *siddiqun*. An overview of Maryam's life in the Qur'an and Islamic traditions indicates clearly that she was in constant contact with the higher realm and in communication with the angels.

The abovementioned verse in Surah al Nisa' speaks of four categories of people that God has blessed: the prophets, the truthful, the witnesses and the righteous.

وَمَن يُطِعِ اللَّهَ وَالرَّسُولَ فَأُوْلَٰٓئِكَ مَعَ الَّذِينَ أَنْعَمَ اللَّهُ عَلَيْهِم مِّنَ النَّبِيِّينَ وَالصِّدِّيقِينَ وَالشُّهَدَاءِ وَالصَّالِحِينَ وَحَسُنَ أُوْلَٰٓئِكَ رَفِيقًا ۞

Whoever obeys God and the Apostle—they are with those whom God has blessed, including the prophets and the truthful, the witnesses and the righteous, and excellent companions are they! (4:69)

Of these four categories of those favoured by God, at least two—'the prophets' and 'the truthful'—are in some sort of contact with God, although the nature of that contact differs. Studying the lives of the prophets before they received revelation, one may conclude that it is only from one of the other three categories of *'the favoured ones'* that God selects His prophets. That is why the prophets were in communication with God even before receiving their mission as is testified by the stories of Prophet Yusuf and Prophet Musa in the Qur'an.

The Shia place their Imams in the category of *siddiqun* and establish the attributes of the *muhaddath* for them. As observed in verse 69 of Surah Nisa, this rank is a category placed immediately after the rank of the prophets. It should be noted that in the Qur'anic context of this verse, the three categories apart from prophethood are technical terms and denote special and incomparable positions and should not be confused with how these terms are used in everyday language.

The *siddiqun* (truthful ones) are above the two other ranks: the witnesses (*shuhada'*) and the righteous (*salihun*), all frequently referred to in the Qur'an. However, it is understood that the members of each higher category include in their excellence all the merits of the lower categories, and therefore, the truthful are the most meritorious among *"those brought near to God"* after the prophets.

Although truthfulness is usually thought of as a quality of speech, actions are also characterized as truthful if they conform to the beliefs and contentions of their actors. This is a higher level of truthfulness. Moreover, sometimes ideas, opinions and intentions might exist or occur in a person's mind that may, unknowingly, falsify their overall belief system. They could arise from doubt, fear, ignorance or some satanic whispering. To avoid such an inconsistency in belief and intention is yet a higher level of truthfulness.

It may be argued that in the Qur'anic technical terminology, the *siddiqun* are those who meet the standards of truthfulness in all these three categories. That is, they are truthful in speech, their actions conform to their words and even their ideas, thoughts and inclinations are in complete harmony with their faith.

The Identity of The Ahlul Bayt

The Shia link the tradition of twelve *khulafa* to another set of reports from the Prophet which speak about the importance of certain members of his family and his descendants, which we refer to here as the Holy Family or Ahlul Bayt. Of course, in general terminology, the Prophet's family was much wider than the venerated Lady Fatima, Imam Ali, Imam Hasan and Imam Hussain. His wives were from his family, as were his uncles and cousins. Loosely speaking, all members of the Prophet's extended family can be included. However, our understanding of the concept changes when the term 'Ahlul Bayt' refers to the divinely-appointed and inspired members of the Prophet's family to whom he alluded on several occasions.

This has always been a point of contention between Sunnis and Shias. The Sunni argument is that the Ahlul Bayt includes the wives of the Prophet. It may also seem strange and contradictory that the Shia regard Imam Ali as part of the Ahlul Bayt but exclude his brother Jafar ibn Abi Talib, the great martyr and pious personality. The Shia would answer that although the prophets have a biological family, they have within that family a smaller chosen group that is considered to be the spiritual family and legators of prophethood. This understanding is confirmed through verses of the Holy Qur'an.

For example, when Prophet Yusuf was a child, his special station above his eleven brothers was evident in his being chosen to be the true successor of his father and his forefathers, Prophet Ishaq and Prophet Ibrahim.

إِذْ قَالَ يُوسُفُ لِأَبِيهِ يَا أَبَتِ إِنِّي رَأَيْتُ أَحَدَ عَشَرَ كَوْكَبًا وَالشَّمْسَ وَالْقَمَرَ رَأَيْتُهُمْ لِي سَاجِدِينَ ۞

قَالَ يَا بُنَيَّ لَا تَقْصُصْ رُؤْيَاكَ عَلَى إِخْوَتِكَ فَيَكِيدُوا لَكَ كَيْدًا إِنَّ الشَّيْطَنَ لِلْانسَانِ عَدُوٌّ مُبِينٌ ۞

وَكَذَالِكَ يَجْتَبِيكَ رَبُّكَ وَيُعَلِّمُكَ مِن تَأْوِيلِ الْأَحَادِيثِ وَيُتِمُّ نِعْمَتَهُ عَلَيْكَ وَعَلَى آلِ يَعْقُوبَ كَمَا أَتَمَّهَا عَلَى أَبَوَيْكَ مِن قَبْلُ إِبْرَاهِيمَ وَإِسْحَاقَ إِنَّ رَبَّكَ عَلِيمٌ حَكِيمٌ ۞

When Yusuf said to his father, 'Father! I saw eleven planets, and the sun and the moon: I saw them prostrating themselves before me,' he said, 'My son, do not recount your dream to your brothers, lest they should devise schemes against you. Satan is indeed man's manifest enemy.' 'That is how your Lord will choose you, and teach you the interpretation of dreams, and complete His blessing upon you and upon the house of Jacob, just as He completed it earlier for your fathers, Abraham and Isaac. Your Lord is indeed all-knowing, all-wise.' (12:4-6)

In Surah Hud, Prophet Nuh laments to God about the perishing of his biological son while God had promised his family would be saved, he was rebuked by God with these words:

$$\text{قَالَ يَا نُوحُ إِنَّهُ لَيْسَ مِنْ أَهْلِكَ إِنَّهُ عَمَلٌ غَيْرُ صَالِحٍ فَلَا تَسْأَلْنِ مَا لَيْسَ لَكَ بِهِ عِلْمٌ إِنِّي أَعِظُكَ أَن تَكُونَ مِنَ الْجَاهِلِينَ}$$

Said He, 'O Nuh! Indeed, He is not of your family. Indeed, he is [a personification of] unrighteous conduct. So do not ask Me [something] of which you have no knowledge. I advise you lest you should be among the ignorant.' (11:46)

Here, God is not casting aspersions on him being the biological son of Prophet Nuh, rather He states he could not be from the spiritual family of Prophet Nuh because of impure deeds while spiritual purity was an essential requirement to repopulate the earth after the great flood. Similarly, there was a wife of Prophet Nuh who was among those who perished. Although they were part of Prophet Nuh's nuclear family, the Qur'an does not include them in the smaller chosen group of his spiritual family.

In the same vein, it would not be possible for all relations of the Prophet to be included among the purified. For example, Abu Lahab, the uncle of the Prophet, was ostentatiously against the prophetic message and the Qur'an. Furthermore, at times, members of the Prophet's household fought against each other, such as in the Battle of Jamal when Aisha, the wife of the Prophet, led an army to fight Imam Ali. The confusion becomes deeper when it is viewed within the context of the Prophetic narration that *"They are always with the Qur'an and do not part."*[55] If they do not part from the Qur'an, then how was it that they fought against each other in a battle in which thousands of Muslims were killed?

One could say that this was because they had different understandings and interpretations of the Qur'an and each worked according to their own *ijtihad* (jurisprudence). However, this would only prove that not everyone in the general family of the Holy Prophet had complete spiritual knowledge, nor were they all divinely-guided.

The Verse of Purity states:

$$\text{إِنَّمَا يُرِيدُ اللَّهُ لِيُذْهِبَ عَنكُمُ الرِّجْسَ أَهْلَ الْبَيْتِ وَيُطَهِّرَكُمْ تَطْهِيرًا}$$

Indeed, God desires to repel all impurity from you, O People of the Household, and purify you with a thorough purification. (33:33)

The interpretation of this verse invokes intense debate between Shia and Sunni schools about why Shia thought does not include the Prophet's wives in this purification despite the initial part of the verse addressing them, as well as the fact that wives are usually considered as part of a household. However, no Sunni scholar denies the fact that Imam Ali, Lady Fatima, Imam Hasan and Imam Hussain are part of the Ahlul Bayt; their argument is that the term should also include the wives and other members of the Prophet's family. As further proof, Sunni scholars quote the another verse in the Qur'an where the term 'Ahlul Bayt' is used which is when the angels brought news of the birth of Prophet Ishaq to the people of the house, which is clearly meant to include both Prophet Ibrahim and his wife Sarah.

$$\text{قَالُوا أَتَعْجَبِينَ مِنْ أَمْرِ اللَّهِ ۖ رَحْمَتُ اللَّهِ وَبَرَكَاتُهُ عَلَيْكُمْ أَهْلَ الْبَيْتِ إِنَّهُ حَمِيدٌ مَجِيدٌ}$$

They said: Do you wonder at God's bidding? The mercy of God and His blessings are on you, **O people of the house**, surely He is Praised, Glorious. (11:73)

The reason for the use of 'Ahlul Bayt' in the above verse is that Sarah was part of the selected Ahlul Bayt of Prophet Ibrahim by virtue of being the mother of Prophet Ishaq, not simply because she was his wife. Historical narrations tell us that Prophet Ibrahim had other wives—and sons by them—after Isma'il and Ishaq, but they are never mentioned as part of his Ahlul Bayt.

There are numerous traditions from both Sunni and Shia sources that the Verse of Purity relates to a particular event when the Prophet took four individuals: Imam Ali, Lady Fatima, Imam Hasan and Imam Hussain under his Yemeni cloak and proclaimed to God that they were his Ahlul Bayt and God in response promised that they were an elite group from whom impurity—in every sense—was to be kept away.[56]

There are even narrations stating that when one of his wives, Umm Salma, asked to join them, the Prophet informed her that she had her own high station but this position was not for her.[57] There are also narrations from the Prophet's wife, Ayesha, confirming the incident of the cloak with none but these five individuals under them.[58]

The fact is that not all members of the Prophet's wider family were cleansed from all impurities, including the darkness of ignorance, which is the most destructive of all. Therefore, only those family members whom the Prophet specifically described, defined and identified for us qualify as the Ahlul Bayt and only they are inspired by divine knowledge. It is these Ahlul Bayt who are the purified ones the Qur'an testifies about as follows:

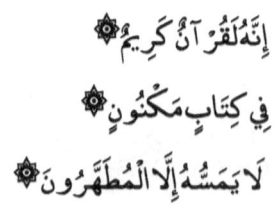

This is indeed a noble Qur'an, in a guarded Book—no one touches it except the pure ones. (56: 77-79)

The "touch" mentioned in this verse does not refer to a physical act. This statement refers to fact that only the purified can grasp the true meanings of the Qur'an because of their divine guidance. None other than the Ahlul Bayt have been accorded this status and neither has anyone else claimed it.

The spiritual position that this purification symbolises is so high that it cannot be fathomed by ordinary people; we have only understood it through explicit statements of the Prophet and of course the Qur'anic verses alluding to those included in this category.

Many companions lived pious lives and sacrificed their lives for Islam; however, they cannot be included in this special category through our judgment and opinion. Imam Ali did not earn his position in the select group of Ahlul Bayt through certain achievements on the battlefield, of which he had plenty. He is in this category because the Prophet proclaimed him to be so, and the Prophet does not speak of his own accord but as a command of God.

Even Lady Zainab and Abul Fadl al Abbas, despite their high standing and knowledge, did not qualify to be in this exclusive category and had to follow their Imam as their *hujjah*. In the same vein, each of the Imams had many children who were pious in their own right; it was only the divinely-chosen among them who qualified to be the Imam of his time in the same way that Prophet Yusuf was divinely-selected above all his brothers.

There are many traditions in both Sunni and Shia sources placing the Ahlul Bayt at the heart of faith. One such tradition is the tradition of *thaqalayn* in which the Prophet said that he was leaving behind two precious things (*thaqalayn*), the Book of God and his Holy Family; another is *Tradition of the Ark:* "*The example of my Ahl al Bayt is like Nuh's ark; whoever boards it is saved and whoever stays behind is drowned.*"[59]

That is why in *Nahjul Balagha*, Imam Ali is reported as saying:

> Have your eyes on the Ahlul Bayt of your Prophet, take their direction and follow their footprints; for they never lead you out of guidance nor take you back to destruction. Thus, if they sit, you (should) sit and if they rise, you (should) rise;

do not move ahead of them for you (would) go astray and do not lag behind them for you (would) perish.[60]

The clear conclusion is that the twelve *khulafa* alluded to in the hadith of the Prophet should uninterruptedly be from the Ahlul Bayt with Imam Mahdi being the twelfth *khalifa*. When Abu al Qasim Ali ibn al Khazzaz al Qummi (d. 400AH) was faced with questions by some Shia that if the institution of the Twelve Imams was so critical, why didn't the Prophet emphasise this, and why are they not included in the Sunni reported traditions on this subject, he was motivated to write his famous book: *Kifayt al athar fi al nass 'ala al a'immatal ithna 'ashar* (Sufficient Amount of Reports Regarding Citation on The Twelve Imams). This book lists more than twenty companions of the Prophet who reported traditions from the Messenger of God on the role of Ahlul Bayt as well as traditions through the chain of our Imams on the matter.

A Summary of the Discussion so far

The hadith corpus from Shia and Sunni schools supports the Qur'anic principles of guidance in building a picture of who the present Imam is, his spiritual position and his centrality to human purpose in the world.

To summarise the discussion so far, Imam Mahdi is the inheritor of the deep knowledge of the Holy Prophet. His spiritual position is that of *hujjatullah* (Proof of God), *khalifatullah* (God's Viceregent) and *muhaddath* (communicator with angels). He is a witness and *siddiq* (truthful and precise in everything). He possesses *hukm*, a divine mandate, and knowledge of the Names. His presence is necessary to uphold the divine connection between the realm of this world and higher worlds without which the purpose of the creation of humanity—which is to be guided towards perfection by God—would vanish. To reiterate, it is not a question of how or whether he is accessible, it is the criticality of his presence in God's divine plan for human creation.

The Prophet spoke of the twelve successors that would follow him and Shias believe them to be the twelve Imams from the Ahlul bayt. Imam Mahdi is the last of these successors and as the following chapters will show, he is recognised as the son of Imam Hasan al Askari who went into hiding in two periods of occultation.

The Identity of the Mahdi

There are ample traditions in highly authentic Shia sources about the identity of the Mahdi as the son of Imam Hassan al Askari. Historically, there has been some confusion, even amongst Shia Muslims themselves, about the identity of the Imams. This is mainly due to the hostile environment that the Imams were living in and the constrictions they faced in the amount of information they could safely impart to their followers. Due to the restrictions of strict dissimulation (*taqiyyah*) and the ban on information-sharing by the Imams themselves (for the protection of their followers), many were not aware that the son of Imam al Askari was the Mahdi even though his name was mentioned by the Holy Prophet himself.

This has led some to argue that the development of twelve Imams was a worried afterthought or a later development in Shia theology. The focus of this section is to look at the evidence that proves that the Mahdi was the son of Imam Hassan al Askari and that the Shias believed right from the beginning that he was the Awaited One.

There are an abundant number of narrations in Shia sources about the identity of Imam Mahdi. Some allude to him by name and others speak of him more vaguely, mentioning characteristics by which people would be able to easily identify him.

Ayatullah Safi Golpaygani has collated 165 traditions that state Imam Mahdi is the ninth descendant of Imam Hussain; 197

traditions that mention him being from the eight descendants of Imam Zayn al Abideen; 121 traditions say he a descendant of Imam Baqir; 112 traditions say that he is the sixth descendant of Imam Jafar al Sadiq; 115 traditions say he is a descendant of Imam Musa al Kadhim; 111 traditions say he is a descendant of Imam al Reza; 107 traditions say he is a descendant of Imam Jawad; 107 traditions say he is a descendant of Imam al Hadi and 108 traditions report that he is the son of Imam Hassan Askari.[61]

An example of such narrations which is reported by Saduq is from Salman al Farsi who said:

> I visited the Prophet while Husayn son of Ali was on his lap. He was kissing his eyes and was saying, 'You are noble, son of a noble, you are Imam, son of an Imam, father of Imams, you are the proof of God, son of His proof and father of nine proofs from your descent, the ninth of whom is their Qaim'.[62]

Several Sunni scholars have reported similar narrations, for example, Abu al Mu'ayyad Muwaffaq al Kharazmi al Hanafi (d. 568 AH) in the seventh chapter of his *Maqtal al Husayn*, which also highlights the merits of Imam Husayn, and al Hafiz al Sheikh Sulayman al Qunduzi al Hanafi in *Yanabi' al mawaddah*. The latter has also reported Imam Husayn's account of the event.[63] Imam al Sajjad reports from his father, Imam al Husayn that he said:

> I visited my grandfather Rasulallah; he put me on his lap and told me, 'God has chosen nine Imams from your descent, the ninth of whom is the Qaim; and all of them are equal in their merits and their position with God.'[64]

A group of these traditions state that the Mahdi is the fourth descendant of Imam al Reza. This is important because Imam al Reza was thought to be the culmination of *Imamah* as he was the crown prince of the Abbasid caliph of the time. Imam al Reza shared the information among his close companions that the

Mahdi would be his fourth descendant.

One of the most explicit of such reports is the account of the visit to Imam al Reza by Di'bil al Khuza'i, a very famous poet who was eventually killed by the Abbasid caliph because of his stance on the Ahlul Bayt. The meeting between Di'bil and Imam al Reza has been reported by both Shia and Sunni scholars.[65]

In this meeting he recited his famous poem, *Madarisu Ayat*:

> *The homes of the Messenger of God are in ruins*
> *While the family of Ziyad dwell in chambers*
> *The family of Ziyad live securely in palaces*
> *while the family of the Messenger of God wander in valleys*

Then after lines of elegy in praise of the Ahlul Bayt, he mentioned the Mahdi in his poem:

> *If it wasn't for what I expect today or tomorrow*
> *My heart would have been cut off for them from sorrow*
> *The emergence of an Imam that will undeniably emerge*
> *Who rises in the name of God with blessings*

At this moment Imam al Reza placed his hand over his head and stood up out of respect and prayed for his (the Mahdi's) arrival. Then he looked at Di'bil and said, "*O Khuza'i, the Holy Spirit (Ruh al Qudus) has spoken these two lines through your tongue. Do you know who this Imam is and when he will rise?*"

Di'bil responded, "*No my Lord, I have only heard from my fathers that an Imam will rise from your family who will fill the earth with equity and justice.*"

Imam al Reza said,

> The Imam after me is my son Muhammad, and after Muhammad will be his son Ali, and after Ali will be his son

> Hasan, and after Hasan will be his son al Hujjat al Qaim. He is the awaited one in his absence, the obeyed one on his return, who will fill the earth with equity and justice after it is filled with injustice and oppression. But to say when he will rise is to foretell the time. Indeed, my father reported to me from his fathers from the Messenger of God that his example is like the example of the Resurrection which does not happen but all of a sudden.[66]

Another group of narrations indicate that he is the grandson of Imam al Hadi, who is quoted to have said, "*The Imam after me is al Hasan, and after al Hasan will be his son al Qaim who will fill the earth with equity and justice after it is filled with injustice and oppression.*"[67]

Muawiyah ibn Hakim, Muhammad ibn Ayyub ibn Nouh and Muhammad ibn Othman al Amri have all said:

> Imam Hasan al Askari showed us his son while we were in his house and said, "This is your Imam after me and my khalifa over you. Obey him and do not divide in your ways after me lest you perish. Beware, you will not see him after this day". They said we left his house, and after a few days, Abu Muhammad passed away.[68]

Traditions about the Occultation

The first Shia book on Imam Mahdi by Fadl Ibn Shadan was written before the death of Imam al Askari, and it reported hadith not only on the twelve Imams but the prophecy about a long occultation long before the event. One of these narrations reported from Imam al Baqir states:

> The Messenger of God said to Ali ibn Abi Talib: "I have more authority on the believers than their own selves; then you, O Ali! have more authority on the believers than their own selves; then al Hasan has more authority on the believers than their own selves; then al Husayn has more authority on the believers than their own selves; then Muhammad ibn 'Ali has more authority on the believers than their own selves; then Ja'far ibn Muhammad has more authority on the believers than their own selves; then Musa ibn Ja'far has more authority on the believers than their own selves; then 'Ali ibn Musa has more authority on the believers than their own selves; then Muhammad ibn 'Ali has more authority on the believers than their own selves; then 'Ali ibn Muhammad has more authority on the believers than their own selves; then al Hasan ibn 'Ali has more authority on the believers than their own selves; then [is] al Hujjat ibn al Hasan with whom the caliphate and successorship will come to end; **and he will remain hidden for a long period of time, then will reappear and fill the earth with justice and equity as it would be full of oppression and injustice."**[69]

Ayatollah Safi Golpaygani in his work *Selected Narrations about the Twelfth Imam*, has collated ten hadith that mention the two occultations; one short and the other long. He has also collected a hundred traditions from our Imams prophesying a long occultation.

Al Kulayni in *al Kafi* and al Tusi in *al Ghaybah* have reported from Imam al Baqir and Imam al Sadiq that they said: "*The* incumbent of this affair will necessarily have a disappearance, and there will be necessarily isolation in his disappearance; however, Medina is a good place of residence and there is no fear among thirty people."[70]

The thirty people referred to here may be those alluded to in the following narration from Imam al Sadiq. *"There will be two occultations for the Qaim, one will be short and the other will be long. In the first occultation, no one will know his whereabouts except the elite of his Shia, in the other one no one knows of his place except the elite of his clients."*[71]

The 'clients' mentioned in the *hadith* above are those who attend to his needs, as per the following narration from Imam al Sadiq: *"No one will be aware of his place, except the client who attends to his needs."*[72]

It is also reported from Imam al Sadiq that, *"The people will lose their Imam; he attends the hajj procession* [mawsim] *and would see them but they don't see him."*[73]

Al Saduq reports from Imam al Sadiq that,

> The incumbent of this affair will have a disappearance from which there is no escape, during which time every deviant will doubt." I asked "Why? May I be your ransom." He said, "For a reason that we are not allowed to disclose to you." I said, "So what is the wisdom behind his disappearance?" He said, "The wisdom behind it would not be revealed until after he reappears; in the same way that the wisdom behind the acts of Khidr [damaging the ship, killing the young boy and erecting the wall] was not revealed to Musa until the time of their departure. O Ibn Fadl! This affair is an affair from [the affairs of] God and a secret from the secrets of God.[74]

Some people have tried to create stories about individuals who have experienced miracles and connected with Imam Mahdi during the major occultation; most of these stories are not reliable. For example, there have been anecdotes of a person lost in a wilderness without food and a man coming to help him and then vanishing. The person assumes this man was the twelfth Imam but has no evidence to suggest it was. The stranger could have been any *waliullah* (friend of God). Such stories may or may not be true, but we should not feel the need to use them to build our faith in the Mahdi.

We have already discussed the necessity of the Imam being present as a *hujjah* (proof) of God on earth, and the reasons behind it, numerous Qur'anic verses, traditions from the Prophet and Imams, confirmation of his noble birth, and proofs during the minor occultation, which leaves no need for such stories to support it.

PART TWO
HIS MISSION

A Contextual Perspective

There are a number of predictions about Imam Mahdi's policies and actions at the time of his reappearance. To properly understand them we must not be limited by a literal understanding of events. This is because some of those mentioned may seem strange when compared to the times we currently living in. Also, the paradigms we refer to now are based on rationality according to our times, whereas we do not know the future political and social paradigms that may exist at the time of his reappearance.

In the same way that our perceptions of the *akhira*—Paradise and Hell — are based on descriptions designed for our current understanding — the reality will be very different; the predictions surrounding reappearance when truthfully realised will have a different reality from our visualizations. For example, concerning Imam Mahdi it was predicted: *"When our Mahdi rises, God will expand the eyes and ears of our followers so that there will be no need for any post between them and the Qaim. He will talk to them from his place and they will see and hear him."*[75]

Another similar prediction states, *"At the time of al Qaim a believer in the east can see his brethren in the west as the one in the west can see his brethren in the east."*[76] Imam al Baqir said, *"The untameable is stored for your man* [al Qaim.]" When asked what the untameable was, he replied, *"He will ride any cloud with thunder, lightning, or thunderbolt."*[77]

Even without the reappearance of the Qaim, we can see how the above predictions may already have been realised through everyday gadgets and technology in so far as the means are concerned. However, this remains vastly different from how people of the past may have imagined it, even as recently as a hundred years ago. Perhaps they gave the above narrations a supernatural meaning or they may have been cynical about how such a matter could ever take place. Technological evolution has changed our paradigms.

With satellite, air travel, the internet and the digital world, we can easily relate to and understand these predictions in a way that we could not have imagined or understood had we not been living in these times.

Knowledge and science are rapidly progressing, and events will occur beyond our present awareness that will change the perceptions of today in unpredictable ways as we have already witnessed through the fulfilled predictions. Thus, any understanding of unfulfilled predictions concerning Imam Mahdi must be viewed whilst keeping this dynamic in mind. The reappearance of Imam Mahdi will put everything in its proper place and conclude it.

Establishing the Book of God

According to the Qur'an and traditions, the primary mission of the Imam is to re-establish the Scripture and faith; to bring to full realisation what the Qur'an sets as the standards of action and justice. In essence, he would bring a renewed life to the Qur'an. According to a narration from Imam Ali in *Nahjul Balagha*: "*He will make desires subservient to guidance while people will have made guidance subservient to desires, and he will make opinions subservient to the Qur'an after the people will have made the Qur'an subservient to their opinions.*"[78]

Society is moving towards secularism, godlessness, and immodesty. Even the religious have developed the tendency to somehow rationalise their thoughts and actions by misrepresenting scripture to suit their modern narratives. We have seen the trend towards making scripture subservient to desire in both Christianity and Islam alike and its effects are becoming apparent in society.

Imam Ali then goes on to speak about the removal of *bid'ah*—innovations in religion—and establishing the *sunnah* (conduct) of the Prophet in its purest form. Speaking about the Mahdi, he said, "*He will remove all unwarranted innovations and will establish all aspects of the sunnah. He will show you the meaning of just governance and will revive what is dead from the Book and the sunnah.*"[79]

This part of the narration has been misunderstood by many to mean that he would bring a new Qur'an, inferring wrongfully through this—and other similarly misunderstood narrations—that the Qur'an in its present form is not complete. This is certainly not the case, the Qur'an remains complete and preserved by the Almighty in the pristine form left to us by the Prophet.

The claim that he will revive what is dead within the Qur'an and *sunnah* means that he will remove errant understandings of the Book and faith. In this way, the Imam will revive the true meanings of faith and give depth to the understanding of the Qur'an and religious practices. He will establish justice in full accordance with Qur'anic precepts, not altered interpretations that have become the cause of dispute for many.

Furthermore, it is vital that the Mahdi revive the different dimensions of guidance in the Qur'an, which have now become dormant within the *ummah*. *Wilayah* is one of these concepts through which we will see our own development and improvement. In this context, Qur'anic verses can be classified into two sections: those that contain potentials that have not yet been realised and those that have remained dormant in the sense that the Prophet and the Imams intended to establish them but people did not allow them.

Foremost among these is justice, which is a paramount concept in the Qur'an but has not yet been recognized either in social or individual application. Establishing justice would therefore be the hallmark of his rule in order to complete the mission of all chosen servants of God before him:

$$\text{لَقَدْ أَرْسَلْنَا رُسُلَنَا بِالْبَيِّنَاتِ وَأَنزَلْنَا مَعَهُمُ الْكِتَابَ وَالْمِيزَانَ لِيَقُومَ النَّاسُ بِالْقِسْطِ}$$

Certainly, We sent Our apostles with manifest proofs and We sent down with them the Book and the Balance, so that mankind may maintain justice. (57:25)

There are, of course, other aspects to the Mahdi's mission and if we were to summarise the traditions concerning those aspects, we could say that he will fully harness the human potential for an increase in faith and reduction of sin; for affluence and a just distribution of wealth and resources throughout the world. He will bring about real security, an expansion in mass knowledge and technology, an enhancement of spiritual capacity and the true faith that the Qur'an continuously stresses; he will arbitrate true peace, universal altruism, appreciation of the environment and the enhancement of life in general.

Waiting for Imam Mahdi

The traditions from Imam Ali also have crucial elements which relate to the concept of *intidhar*, waiting for the Imam. These will be discussed in the following section on our responsibility whilst preparing for his return, including the qualities that are required from us individually and as a society.

The ten aspects of his rule that we shall discuss in the next chapter are the most salient aspects of faith that we currently do not pay proper attention to. Faith is not simply praying and fasting and rituals; it is far vaster in reality and this is what the Imam is going to revive.

One might question why God did not allow these merits to manifest at the beginning of time instead of at the end of it. As with everything in His divine plan, this chronology of events is for human beings to realise for themselves that justice is the pivotal concept of all existence and that it can be accomplished with the right leadership.

قُلْ فَلِلَّهِ الْحُجَّةُ الْبَالِغَةُ فَلَوْ شَاءَ لَهَدَاكُمْ أَجْمَعِينَ ۞

Say, 'To God belongs the conclusive argument. Had He wished, He would have surely guided you all.' (6:149)

This verse states that the effective argument is for God, and He will bring about its conclusion before the culmination of the human race and the Day of Judgement. Even though we possessed the *potential* from the beginning of time to obey in a manner that would lead to the fulfilment of the promises in the Qur'an, the free will that God has given mankind did not allow Him to force His Will in this matter. The choice to deviate has always been ours.

Surah Fussilat states:

إِنَّ الَّذِينَ يُلْحِدُونَ فِي آيَاتِنَا لَا يَخْفَوْنَ عَلَيْنَا أَفَمَنْ يُلْقَىٰ فِي النَّارِ خَيْرٌ أَمْ مَنْ يَأْتِي آمِنًا يَوْمَ الْقِيَامَةِ اعْمَلُوا مَا شِئْتُمْ إِنَّهُ بِمَا تَعْمَلُونَ بَصِيرٌ ۞

Those who abuse Our signs are not hidden from Us. Is someone who is cast in the Fire better off or someone who arrives safely on the Day of Resurrection? Act as you wish; indeed, He watches what you do. (41:40)

Despite our freedom to act, the legislative will of God and His promise must also come to pass before we can proceed to the next stage towards Him. For this reason, the arrival of Imam Mahdi also signals the end of the human race. This is also explained by a statement of Imam Ali: *"With our Mahdi ['s appearance], all arguments would be ineffective; for he is the last Imam, the saviour of the 'Ummah, and the highest point of light, and has abstruse secrets."*[80] Imam Ali says that "all arguments will be ineffective" meaning no one will have any argument or excuse against God after the coming of the Mahdi as he will bring about circumstances and proofs that will negate them all.

There are some promises in the Qur'an that remain unfulfilled or rather they have not found any grounds for fulfilment. Close attention to these verses shows that these too will be satisfied when the Mahdi establishes his society. One example is:

وَلَوْ أَنَّ أَهْلَ الْقُرَىٰ آمَنُوا وَاتَّقَوْا لَفَتَحْنَا عَلَيْهِم بَرَكَاتٍ مِّنَ السَّمَاءِ وَالْأَرْضِ وَلَٰكِن كَذَّبُوا فَأَخَذْنَاهُم بِمَا كَانُوا يَكْسِبُونَ ۞

If the people of the towns had been faithful and God wary, We would have opened to them blessings from the heavens and the earth. But they denied so We seized them because of what they used to earn. (7:96)

God says that if there was a global community in which faith prevailed, He would open the gates of His *barakah* (treasures). Some question why He has filled the earth with so many resources, but given us access to comparatively little. The Qur'an explains:

وَلَوْ بَسَطَ اللَّهُ الرِّزْقَ لِعِبَادِهِ لَبَغَوْا فِي الْأَرْضِ وَلَٰكِن يُنَزِّلُ بِقَدَرٍ مَّا يَشَاءُ إِنَّهُ بِعِبَادِهِ خَبِيرٌ بَصِيرٌ ۞

Were God to expand the provision for [all] His servants, they would surely create havoc on the earth. But He sends down in a [precise] measure whatever He wishes. Indeed, He is All-Aware, All-Seeing about His servants. (42:27)

Humanity as a community is still not ready to receive these treasures in abundance, because we have not yet obeyed, and the reform of the Mahdi has not taken place. We can observe how much arrogance, greed, bloodshed, and injustice exist on Earth with the blessings we have already. If these blessings were bestowed on us before our communal reform, we would create more havoc on Earth. This is why the change has to come from within us, under the guidance of the Mahdi, before God's promise can be qualified.

Similarly in Surah Jinn, God says:

$$وَأَنْ لَوِ اسْتَقَامُوا عَلَى الطَّرِيقَةِ لَأَسْقَيْنَاهُمْ مَاءً غَدَقًا ۞$$

If they are steadfast on the path [of God], We shall provide them with abundant water. (72:16)

God promises the jinn abundant water if they are steadfast on His path. "Water" here is an analogy for sustenance (*rizq*) and from traditions, we are told that abundance is the prevalent feature of the Mahdi's time. Traditions mention that people will search for anyone to give charity to without success.[81] Other hadith go as far as to say that if someone goes to the Mahdi asking for something he will offer them double what they ask. However, let us remember to be careful not to take these words too literally and focus instead on the concept of abundance in his time.

Our economies today are all based on scarcity and the distribution of limited resources.

Abundance will need a drastically different economic model. It is difficult to imagine a system based on the distribution of abundant goods. How would we utilise the surplus? How would it affect production techniques and technology? What new products could it give rise to?

Presently, disbelief or incorrect beliefs are more prominent in society than truth and faith. During the rule of Imam Mahdi, disbelief will not disappear, but it will not be the salient aspect of life. Life will be lived according to the one true faith. Of course, the people in that society will have a greater advantage in guidance than we do in the same way that we have an advantage over those born before the time of Prophet Mohammed. God will judge everyone according to their circumstances.

The Mahdi's mission is to realise the Prophetic mission which is the fulfilment of Qur'anic precepts. There is no difference between his mission and that of Prophet Muhammad. He will not add anything new; he will only bring forth the true *shariah* of the Prophet as it was intended. There is exceptional support from God for the Mahdi and his mission, for the reasons explained earlier. Therefore, with His divine help, factors that were allowed to play out earlier in the case of prophets and other Imams will not be allowed to succeed.

The Defining Features of His Time

In this chapter, we will attempt to analyse the defining features of the rule of Imam Mahdi.

1. Justice

The Prophet is widely reported to have said, "*The (Final) Hour will not pass before a man from my Ahlul Bayt will rule the earth filling it with justice after it is filled with oppression. He will rule for seven years.*"[82]

The "Hour" referred to in the hadith is the Day of Judgement and "ruling the earth" means everyone will obey Imam Mahdi. The continuation of the hadith says he will rule for seven years. however, we must bear in mind that there are contradictory narrations regarding the duration of his rule, therefore seven years or any term is not important for the purposes of our understanding. The important point here is that the hallmark of his rule is that it "*fills the earth with justice after it is filled with oppression.*"

In another hadith, Abu Said al Khudri narrated from the Prophet that: "*I give you good tidings about the Mahdi. He will rise in my ummah during shocking division among people. Then he will fill the earth with justice and equity after it is filled with oppression and corruption. The inhabitants of the heavens and the earth are pleased with him. He will distribute wealth rightly.*" Someone asked, "What is meant by rightly?" He replied, "*Equally.*"[83]

The "shocking division" in this hadith refers to huge, catastrophic events that shake the world and humanity. In the Qur'an, the term *zilzal* is used, meaning earth-shaking. It is repeated here that "*he will fill the earth with justice and equity after it is filled with oppression and corruption.*" Also, that "*the inhabitants of the heavens and the earth are pleased with him.*" This may mean people of other planets as there are allusions in the Qur'an that there are other living beings on other planets. This is of course an equivocal expression because *sakin us sama* (the inhabitants of the heavens) can also refer to angels.

The Prophet clarified that there will be equal distribution of wealth. Equality is a sensitive term as one might question the basis on which people are treated equally. There is a third hadith quoted in *Bihar al Anwar*: "*By God, his justice enters inside their homes as enters heat and cold.*"[84] Countless narrations, both in Shia and Sunni sources, refer to the Mahdi filling the earth with justice after it has been filled with oppression.

Justice is such a fundamental in Islam and to the rule of Imam Mahdi that Imam Ali describes it in the following words when speaking of Imam Mahdi's advent:

> Islam and a just ruler are two brothers who are always together. One cannot be corrected without the other. Islam is the foundation and the just ruler is the protector. What is without a foundation will be destroyed and what is without a protector will be spoiled.[85]

Justice has been defined in narrations to mean 'to place everything in its proper position.' We currently observe that there is already so much injustice in the world that we might question whether it is not already full to the brim with oppression, and how will the Imam bring about such a major change?

Whilst it is true that injustices are increasing by the day, we must be careful to recognize that there are still some redeeming factors as well. The scale of injustice may be vastly different before the Mahdi's reappearance. Although values are evolving and many of them are not consistent with Islamic or spiritual values, there are still some positive manifestations.

A world 'filled with injustice' implies a place where people cannot tolerate living. We must be careful not to let our imagination dominate the understanding of his re-appearance—it may be now or tomorrow, close, or far—we do not really know when the time will actualise. There have been events in the past where people hastily interpreted traditions and concluded that there had been a definite sign of the Imam's reappearance and they were wrong, which led to further disappointment. In fact, in the 13th century CE, when the Mongols ransacked and pillaged through lands, people thought they were the Yagug and Majuj that have been prophesied!

All we should take from the traditions is that injustice will be pervasive, suffocating and make everyone on earth uncomfortable.

2. Increase in faith and reduction of sin

The second outcome of the Imam's re-appearance is that faith will increase and naturally, sins will reduce. One reason for this may be that people will have learned of the negative effects of faithlessness from their experience of terrible injustices, greed, oppression, chaos and grief. Through the guidance of the Imam, they will be looking for renewed hope and strength, that can only come from spirituality and faith. One narration states that:

> Evil will go away and good will persist. Man will plant one mudd[86] and harvest seven as [the verse of] God Almighty says. Fornication, drinking and usury will vanish, and people will turn to worship, law, religiosity and praying in congregation. Lives will be prolonged, trusted goods will be returned, trees will bear fruit, the evil ones will perish and the good ones remain. There will be no one who would hate the Ahlul Bayt.[87]

People will realise the consequences of sin and will be wary of indulging in them again. It is this common human realisation that will catalyse human transformation towards faith and obedience. That is why, as the tradition states, "evil will go away and good will persist." It will be a gradual transformative realisation rather than some magical change that happens with the wave of a wand. Imam Mahdi would certainly be the agent for the removal of obstacles, however, actual change will need to be an organic progressive growth within the heart of humankind. This is also why certain events must happen before this realisation takes hold and the evil of faithlessness is laid bare.

Humanity is currently rushing towards self-destruction. The wonders of science and technological advancement have not brought us closer to the truth as we had anticipated. Instead, they have rendered us arrogant so that we feel needless of God. Humanity must come to its own realisation that this is wrong and that we must go back to faith; this is the only way for evil to disappear and good to persist.

In the time of the Mahdi, fornication, usury, drunkenness and other vices will lose their appeal and be discarded. Instead, people will turn to religiosity and worship. Lives will be long. Trust will be established. Trees will be fruitful. The evil will perish and the good remain. There will be no one who will be ignorant of the Ahlul bayt or hate them. This is because when Imam Mahdi returns, the world will be attracted to his character and his message; in learning about the Ahlul Bayt, they will love them and everything they stand for.

We cannot emphasize enough the importance of keeping in mind that all this will be part of a process. Not everyone will follow him the moment he re-appears; in fact, some might wish to cause him harm or fight him. However, he will succeed in winning over the majority who will understand and accept the realities of life as he will explain them.

3. Affluence

The traditions state that when the Mahdi comes: "*Lives will be prolonged, trusted goods are returned, trees bear fruit.*"

The verses of the Qur'an quoted earlier indicated that if people had piety (*taqwa*), the blessings (*barakat*) from the heavens and the earth would come to them. The implication was that if they were given these blessings without faith, it would lead them to transgression. With the transformation of the human soul and its spiritual ascension, there would be no need for strict control of provisions and blessings. We can imagine that in the current times, if the wealth of this world was increased exponentially, it would only benefit a select few—the powerful, the greedy and the selfish; a blessing would turn into a curse.

At the time of the Mahdi, there will be no reason to restrict provisions and blessings and affluence will be widespread. In a tradition, Abu Saeed al Khudri narrates from the Prophet: "*Both righteous and wicked will enjoy such comfort at his time as they have never experienced the like of. The sky will pour [rain] over them in abundance and the earth will bring out its vegetation.*"[88]

The interesting point in the above narration is the acknowledgement of the existence of wicked people even during the time of the Mahdi. It might be tempting to assume that there would be no disbelievers once the truth has been made clear and that everyone will become good. This is not realistic. There will be wicked people, but they will be under the control of the good whereas throughout history—and in the present time as well—it has always been the opposite.

It is important to point this out because free will never be suppressed. If we presume that everyone should become pious by the force of Imam Mahdi then God's system of human free will and testing in this life would be negated. Consequently, there will be wicked people, but they too will benefit from a standard of living that they cannot currently access even as rulers or powerful people. At the time of the Imam, they will be in a harmonious environment under righteous leadership; thus, the benefits of a just society will be obvious even to them.

Jabir has narrated a tradition from Imam al Baqir which explains this phenomenon.

> The whole wealth of the world, both inside and outside the earth, will be brought to him. He will say to people, come and take from that for which you shed blood and cut your relations and committed what God had forbidden. So, he will give in such a way that no one before him has ever given.[89]

With the treasures of the earth—its minerals, metals, crops, fruit—and the treasures of the seas—known and unknown—at the disposal of the human race under the leadership of the Imam, one of the major factors of diversion will be destroyed. Often, due to the unfairness of the systems we live in, the motivation for stealing, embezzling, corruption and bloodshed stems from the need to fulfil a basic requirement or to fill a void within a person where something is lacking. During the government of the Imam, people will be content and happy; these feelings are so fulfilling that even the wicked will find no reason to oppose this benevolent system.

Another hadith states from the Prophet that:

> My ummah will enjoy such comfort at his time as they have never experienced before. The earth will expose its fruits and would not keep any treasure away from them. The wealth will be piled up in a way that a man would go to the Mahdi and say give me, and he will say, take (what you wish).[90]

The spirit of the narration suggests that there will be such an abundance of wealth that a person's request will not be denied. Again, we must go beyond the literal and anticipate that the actual economical system will be extremely sophisticated to allow this state of abundance to persist.

There are two important narrations from Imam al Sadiq:

> He will judge (with the) the judgment of Dawud and Muhammad; as a result, the earth will throw out its treasures and manifest its blessings; on that day not one of you will find a recipient for his charity as prosperity will embrace all the believers.[91]

and

> The earth will throw out its treasures in a way that people will see it on its surface, and you will look for someone to give him benevolently or to take your zakat from you but will not find anyone. People will become needless because of what God has provided for them from His bounties.[92]

From these narrations, we can deduce that poverty will vanish, and that the judgements of the Mahdi will be made with the wisdom and justice of Prophet Dawud and Prophet Mohammed. These narrations all point to an economic model that will be independent of supply and demand, pricing and distribution.

In light of how human society has been trained to think, whether it be in terms of capitalism or socialism, how will economic activity manifest when there is an abundance of resources and wealth being distributed according to people's wants and desires? Will there still be a need for employment and jobs? Will factories continue production? Will it be like a universal benefit system where people stay at home and receive their wealth? How would such an idle society advance?

Perhaps human beings would continue in their efforts, but according to a new social and economic model, taking inspiration and motivation from the new paradigm in which they would find themselves. In the current models of society, we work for money; in the model of Imam Mahdi, perhaps it would be for our personal fulfilment and growth in capacity, as a human duty.

We see scattered instances of this in our current times; some people pursue knowledge not to increase their earnings but to satisfy their innate desire for personal development. Karl Marx, in his theory of socialism, said that work is fulfilling for workers because that is how they discover their identity. Without work, human beings would be alienated from themselves. He argued that the right to work is essential for every human. His theory was that, if socialism prevailed, people would not need to work long hours and would use their spare time to educate themselves. The contradiction in Marx's theory, however, is that if people find personal fulfilment through work and then reduce it gradually over time, that would slow their growth towards that very identity and personal fulfilment.

Instead of focusing on personal development alone, the work ethic should be viewed within a social context. The aspiration for altruism and peace of mind that comes from serving others is within us all. Perhaps a person's primary motivation will also change when they are satisfied by using their skills for the betterment of others and not only themselves. More importantly, people would then have time to dedicate to worship and remembrance of God which is the essential purpose of human life on earth.

At the time of Imam Mahdi, people will continue to strive to work and educate themselves, but their motivation will be for the greater good. They will have more time for worship and capacity-building for the life to come. Resources will not be wasted on personal whims or wrongful pleasures. The economic effort would be based not on competing for resources but on sharing them within a harmonious and just society.

To illustrate this further, imagine a society where everything is free. At first, people would rush to get their shares of the booty before it runs out. This is a natural reaction because of the present economy of scarcity that makes us all greedy and acquisitive. But if over time, people become accustomed to the idea that everything they need is abundant and freely accessible, then their attitude and behaviour will change. Human behaviour will adapt as there would be no need, even for the wicked, to exercise foul means to acquire anything despite a proclivity to do so. In essence, evil will become disincentivised.

To look at it from another perspective we can ask ourselves: why do angels work? Is it because God commands them to do so? That would not be an accurate answer. The reality is that they work because their functions are part of their identity, their self-actualisation lies within those functions. Even Heaven is not a place where we will be simply reclining and eating all the time, we will have functions to perform to continuously actualise our identities, as part of our continuous movement towards our Creator.

It may be very difficult for us to imagine such a society as it sounds almost like a fairy tale. Many man-made systems have claimed to have the answers to the realisation of this utopia, but they have failed. This situation will nevertheless come to realisation by Divine Promise and decree for the reasons already enumerated in the previous chapter. This will not happen, of course, without the chaos and struggle preceding it.

4. Security

The natural outcome of an affluent society will be a sense of security. The following Qur'anic verse in Surah Nur, accepted by the overwhelming majority of the commentators of the Qur'an to be relating to the time of the Mahdi, confirms this.

وَعَدَ اللَّهُ الَّذِينَ آمَنُوا مِنكُمْ وَعَمِلُوا الصَّالِحَاتِ لَيَسْتَخْلِفَنَّهُمْ فِي الْأَرْضِ كَمَا اسْتَخْلَفَ الَّذِينَ مِن قَبْلِهِمْ وَلَيُمَكِّنَنَّ لَهُمْ دِينَهُمُ الَّذِي ارْتَضَىٰ لَهُمْ وَلَيُبَدِّلَنَّهُم مِّن بَعْدِ خَوْفِهِمْ أَمْنًا يَعْبُدُونَنِي لَا يُشْرِكُونَ بِي شَيْئًا وَمَن كَفَرَ بَعْدَ ذَٰلِكَ فَأُولَٰئِكَ هُمُ الْفَاسِقُونَ ۞

God has promised those of you who have faith and do righteous deeds that He will surely make them successors on the earth, just as He made those who were before them successors, and He will surely establish for them their religion which He has approved for them, and that He will surely change their state to security after their fear, while they worship Me, not ascribing any partners to Me. Whoever is ungrateful after that—it is they who are the transgressors. (24:55)

A narration in this regard explains: "*Grudges and enmity will leave the hearts, and the beasts of prey and the livestock will live in peace. So much so that a woman will travel between Iraq and Syria and not step but on green vegetation and will have all her ornaments on her without fearing a beast attacking her.*"[93]

Once the need to compete for resources is removed, then jealousy and its manifestations will also fade away. People's behaviour towards each other will be more loving and tolerant. Some aspects of the narration above need to be taken in their figurative sense, especially about animals living in peace with each other. This is because they still need to hunt and eat to fulfil their natural dispositions. The last example in the tradition about a woman being able to travel alone through lush vegetation underlines both the changes in the earth and in the animalistic behaviour of mankind.

Imam al Sadiq is reported to have said: "*When our Qaim rises, he will rule with justice; inequity will be removed in his days; the roads will be secure; the earth will reveal its blessings; he will restore every right to their owners.*"[94]

Security will be a global phenomenon. An overwhelming sense of protection will prevail. This is not simply the result of satiation from material needs, it will also be due to the enhancement of society's spiritual capacity and the swift enforcement of justice.

5. The Growth of Knowledge

Knowledge will expand exponentially during the time of the Mahdi. This will be in all subjects, from mathematics and physics to social and human sciences. More importantly, intellectual faculties and true spiritual intellect will develop and manifest in ways that do not exist today. Society and individuals will not only become aware of the true meaning of knowledge but have access to the practical steps on how to achieve it. This is demonstrated in the following tradition from Imam al Baqir: "*When our Qaim rises, he will put his hand over people's heads by which he will complete their intellects and will perfect their traits.*"[95]

In another hadith, he says, "*You will be given wisdom in his time to the extent that a lady will judge among people in her house according to the Book of God and the sunnah of the Prophet.*"[96] These traditions speak of both knowledge and moral traits reaching their peak. Of course, "putting his hand over their heads" is a metaphor for overseeing human development as an Imam and guide.

The statement in this tradition about a lady judging in her house is very interesting. We could perhaps infer that differences among people would be resolved within homes, based on divine precepts thereby dispensing with the need for courts, lawyers or arbitrators. That would be the prevailing level of wisdom.

This does not mean that criminal or immoral acts will not be committed at all. The narration is referring to an environment where justice is swift, and judgements are not arbitrary. Also, when analysing the statement about women judging, we must take it in the context of the low levels of education amongst women at the time the hadith was narrated. Today, education is available in developed countries to both men and women and in a way, this allows us to understand the hadith better and see how we are getting closer to these predictions already.

Similarly, Imam Jaffar al Sadiq narrates that: *"When our Qaim rises, God will extend for our Shia their hearing and their vision to the extent that there will be no need for the post between them and the Qaim. He will talk from his place and they will hear him and will look at him."* This seems to be a condition precedent that has already been realised in our time.

Overall, we are already witnessing rapid growth in knowledge. Ideas like stem cell technology and Artificial Intelligence that belonged in science fiction novels just a few decades ago are already becoming part of our daily realities. One can only imagine how advanced society might be at the time of the Imam.

Diseases we battle today could be completely curable and even eradicated as medical research continues to advance. Although this is the trajectory we are moving towards, when the Imam comes this inquest into the world of creation will become more profound. Some may say that these advancements are problematic because they tamper in the creational realm, which is God's domain. In discussing the ethics of scientific advancements and abilities, we need to bear in mind that firstly God's powers are incomprehensible and infinite; any human advancement is absolutely insignificant and hardly comparable. Secondly, humans, as the children of Adam, have been endowed with the potential to gain access to higher realms of knowledge. This ability is what sets us apart from the rest of creation in our collective role of *khalifatullah*.

Therefore, we can advance in this way only because God Himself has allowed it or given us the capacity to do so. Our discoveries are supposed to bring us closer to understanding Him. Imam al Sadiq has said, *"Knowledge is 27 letters; all that the prophets have brought with them are two letters, so the people do not know until this day but those two. When our Qaim rises he will bring out the other 25 letters and will disseminate them among the people and will add to them the other two to spread the whole 27 letters."*[97]

This hadith can be used to understand both material and spiritual knowledge. The scale and scope of spiritual insight and knowledge about God that will prevail at the time of the Mahdi cannot be fully grasped. To further underline the impact of this tradition in driving human change towards betterment, we must remember that knowledge as the source of good is a constant theme in the Qur'an and traditions, and that ignorance has always been cited as the cause of many evils. In *Nahj al Balaghah*, Imam Ali says about this time to come:

> He will be in concealment from the people. The stalker will not find his footprints even though he pursues them with his eyes. Then a group of people will be sharpened like the sharpening of swords by the blacksmith. Their sight will be brightened by revelation, the [delicacies of] commentary will be put in their ears and they will be given drinks of wisdom morning and evening.[98]

6. One Faith

The Mahdi will bring about a return to the one true faith, that God has decreed for mankind. There has always been only one religion of God that has been preached by all the prophets, but people tampered with faith to suit their inclinations and became divided. Christianity, Judaism and other faiths like Buddhism and Hinduism have transformed so greatly from their origins that they are no longer recognisable from their monotheistic roots. They all emanated from a single faith and a universal set of principles, but the followers of the prophets made misguided modifications in revelation and faith that took them away from the truth.

The verses in the Surah Aal Imran and Surah Mu'minoon testify:

$$إِنَّ الدِّينَ عِندَ اللَّهِ الْإِسْلَامُ ۗ وَمَا اخْتَلَفَ الَّذِينَ أُوتُوا الْكِتَابَ إِلَّا مِن بَعْدِ مَا جَاءَهُمُ الْعِلْمُ بَغْيًا بَيْنَهُمْ ۗ وَمَن يَكْفُرْ بِآيَاتِ اللَّهِ فَإِنَّ اللَّهَ سَرِيعُ الْحِسَابِ ۞$$

Indeed, with God religion is *islam*, and those who were given the Book did not differ except after knowledge had come to them, out of envy among themselves. And whoever denies God's signs [should know that] God is swift at reckoning. (3:19)

$$فَتَقَطَّعُوا أَمْرَهُم بَيْنَهُمْ زُبُرًا ۖ كُلُّ حِزْبٍ بِمَا لَدَيْهِمْ فَرِحُونَ ۞$$

But they fragmented their religion among themselves, each party boasting about what it had. (23:53)

People have torn apart this one faith into different faiths, with every follower or every faith satisfied in their own adapted versions. These differences in understanding will be eradicated by the Mahdi and there will be one faith: *islam*.

Imam al Sadiq said, "*O Mufaddal, I swear by God that all differences between religions and creeds will disappear, and the faith will be one as God the Mighty Glorified has said: 'The religion with God is only islam.'*"[99]

Miqdad reports from the Prophet that: "*There will remain no house or tent on the face of the earth unless God will bring into it the kalimah of Islam.*"[100]

The move to the one true faith will not occur by force, it never has. There will initially be a dialogue between faiths, especially

Christianity, Judaism, and Islam—the Abrahamic faiths. The most obvious unification will be after Prophet Isa arrives and supports Imam Mahdi, upon which the Christians will become one with Muslims.

7. Prevalence of Peace

In today's world, true peace is an illusion. We need war as a deterrence and to—ironically—'keep the peace', due to the numerous differences between ourselves. All despite the fact that this deterrent could endanger the whole of humanity. After the advent of the Mahdi and the stability he will bring to society, this elusive peace will finally change to a real peace.

Imam Ali is reported to have said, *"When our Qaim rises, the sky sends down its rain and the earth brings out its crops and the hatred and enmity leaves the heart of people."*[101]

This is an allusion to the general global environment. This will not be the case for the individual hearts of the wicked, who will exist although only God knows why they will continue in their wickedness while there is no reason for it anymore.

8. Universal Altruism

The Mahdi will bring about a society with so much external and internal improvement that people will give precedence to the needs of others before thinking about themselves.

The Holy Prophet is reported to have said:

> He casts compassion and mercy between them, so they prefer others over themselves and distribute (wealth) equally; the poor becomes needless; no one is superior over others; the old have mercy over the young and the young honour the old. They believe in haqq (truth) and act and judge based on that.[102]

The "poor" referred to in this tradition refers to those before the advent of the Imam because at the time of the Imam there will be no poverty. There will be no sense of superiority and people will witness and experience the true sense of humanity; everyone will want to help others, to fulfil something in themselves.

9. Care for Nature

It is not just the people, but the planet itself that will benefit from the return of the Imam. One tradition states: "*He will fill the earth with justice after it is filled with oppression. During his reign the inhabitants of the earth and the inhabitants of the heavens and the birds in the air will be pleased.*" The inhabitants of the heavens could refer to beings from other planets or angels. The overarching idea though is that care for the environment and nature is part of the system of prosperity that the Imam will bring.

A narration from Imam al Baqir states: "*There will remain no desolate place on the earth unless it is built.*"[103] This means that the earth will become habitable with its natural beauties fully presenting themselves. Issues of environmental destruction, pollution and climate change will all be rectified. One can only envision what kind of damage will have been done by then as a result of wars and corporate greed.

10. Enhancement of life

Enhancement of life in general and health will be another aspect of the Imam's mission. People will have better health, and illnesses, plagues and pandemics will lessen. A narration goes as far as to say, "*No blind, crippled or disease-afflicted will be found on earth.*"[104]

This will obviously be due to the advancement of human knowledge and sciences that will follow his lead. For every disease, there is a medicine—we just have to discover it. Even today we hear of organ transplants, gene therapy, and stem cell transplant that were not considered possible a few years ago. The time of Imam Mahdi will bring with it the peak of medical knowledge and ability and advances in curing illnesses will be a natural result of that.

Living healthy in that time does not mean that one can live forever, although people may have a greater life expectancy. However, the hadith concentrates more on the quality of life with good physical and spiritual—without disease or disability—than a guaranteed life span.

We must also think about the capacity of the globe to sustain the needs of the population. Today one sees 'rich' countries concerned with population growth in poorer countries because they fear they will not be able to sustain the expanding population. Presently the earth is feeding 8 billion people in an unequal manner, so the capacity is present. At the time of the advent, with fair wealth distribution and improvement in resource management, perhaps it can feed 80 billion people! In today's capitalist models of society, this is a very difficult future to envision and those who offer such an alternative perspective are often called foolish because people cannot let go of their present perceptions.

Active Hope for the Ease (*Faraj*)

All the features listed above are aspects of a utopian-like society that may seem too good to be true. Even if we cannot imagine such a future, God does not break His promise and it will come to pass:

$$\text{وَتَمَّتْ كَلِمَتُ رَبِّكَ صِدْقًا وَعَدْلًا ۚ لَا مُبَدِّلَ لِكَلِمَاتِهِ ۚ وَهُوَ السَّمِيعُ الْعَلِيمُ}$$

The word of your Lord has been fulfilled in truth and justice. Nothing can change His words, and He is the All-Hearing, the All-Knowing. (6:115)

Observing the state of the world around us today, we may still wonder exactly how such a society might come about. The advancements in the various fields of science and technology so far have more often been used to promote injustices rather than make peace in the world. This will probably continue to happen until humanity reaches the peak of this self-destructive process. This will be when mankind finally realises the impact the false constructs in society have had.

When the global community realises its past mistakes and begins to crave change and a new beginning, the time will be prime for the Mahdi to return and lead us towards our true purpose. Humanity is destined for something much greater than what we are currently experiencing. Knowledge, progress and everything in the Universe are all manifestations of the Names (*asm'a*) of God. We were created and destined to possess this knowledge.

It is a lack of faith that does not allow us to use our knowledge correctly and thus fail at becoming *khalifatullah*. The Imam will come to teach us the way to find this path of faith so that we can claim our full human potential and undertake our final journey on this earth. This will be the realisation that Prophet Nuh beseeched God for many thousands of years ago:

فَقُلْتُ اسْتَغْفِرُوا رَبَّكُمْ إِنَّهُ كَانَ غَفَّارًا ۝

يُرْسِلِ السَّمَاءَ عَلَيْكُمْ مِدْرَارًا ۝

وَيُمْدِدْكُمْ بِأَمْوَالٍ وَبَنِينَ وَيَجْعَلْ لَكُمْ جَنَّاتٍ وَيَجْعَلْ لَكُمْ أَنْهَارًا ۝

Plead to your Lord for forgiveness. Indeed, He is All-Forgiving. Then He will send for you abundant rains from the sky, and aid you with wealth and sons, and provide you with gardens and provide you with streams. (71:10-12)

It is in the interest of all of humanity for the Mahdi to return as soon as possible. Although his mission seems challenging—almost impossible—it is destined by God and He will help the Mahdi achieve all that has been discussed above and more, beyond our expectations. We pray for his quick and safe arrival and that we can be part of the revolution that brings about so much positive development in the world.

PART THREE
OUR RESPONSIBILITIES

The Leading Imam

It is important to understand how we view the Imam in the context of our personal responsibility. What are our duties? Should we be worried that he hasn't manifested himself until now? Is it better to live now in this situation or at the time of his re-appearance?

There certainly are responsibilities for a believer during the time of occultation that we must be conscious of and also great merits of living during this period. Many traditions speak very highly about believers who maintain their faith, practices and conviction during this time and of the rewards and status they will achieve. Maintaining a strong belief in an Imam who is not physically present is difficult and God always compensates for any disadvantages.

Before we delve into the traditions referred to above, we must understand that even if we lived in the times of the Imams preceding Imam Mahdi, it would have been an era in which even the Imam would have been awaiting the rise of the Qaim (the One that Rises). Our preceding Imams did not have the political power or social freedom that would allow their followers full access to them. For example, Imam Hasan al Askari was under house arrest in a garrison town and only a few people could contact him; those that did manage to see him brought back conflicting news and reports from him. He had no material power or means to effect societal change.

Therefore, the conditions of the community living at the time when the Imams were present such as Imam al Askari, Imam al Kadhim or Imam al Jawad were not very different to present times. The believers in those times are regarded to be like us. The main function of an Imam is to lead society. When an Imam is present but unable to lead, a vacuum exists similar to our current situation. This is why there are many traditions from the Imams speaking about 'when the Qaim comes' without specifying further. They kept the identity of the Qaim vague in many of the traditions and mentioned him as the "twelfth" in many others. In most traditions, they were careful not to mention the identity of the Qaim.

Sometimes the Shia of the past were treated in their own times as a people without an Imam due to the suffocating political environment that highly restricted their contact with their leader. Our present dilemma is worse because we have no contact whatsoever with our Imam. It is important to keep this point in mind when analysing relevant traditions on the subject that we will quote below.

The first hadith relates to a conversation between the Prophet and Imam Ali. The Prophet said to him: "*The people of greatest certitude are a people who will be at the end of the time; they did not catch up with the Prophet, and the hujjah would be veiled from them. So, they believed in some black on white.*"[105]

This hadith can refer to all believers after the time of the major occultation, who could not meet the Prophet or any of the Imams. The "belief in black on white" alludes to beliefs formed through the study of Scripture and traditions. Their faith is based on the unseen, in the sense that they have not seen the Prophet or any of the Imams yet they are strong in faith.

The believers at the time of the previous Imams were often faced with contradicting positions of constant doubt and hesitation. They fluctuated from one side to another, losing faith and certainty (*yaqeen*) in the process. Compared to them, there are believers today who do not see their Imam, but display a steady strength in their faith. This is why the Prophet had been quoted to have said that they are the ones with the greatest certitude when compared to many of the companions of the Prophet or those of the Imams. Imam al Sadiq also alluded to this when answering a question from one of his followers who asked about his opinion concerning a person who dies on the conviction of 'this matter'. He said, "*He is like the one who is with the Qaim in his very tent.*" Then he paused for a moment and said, "*He is like someone who was with the Messenger of God.*"[106]

Usually, the Imams applied the vague term *hadhal amr* (this matter) to mean the matter of *wilayah* (divine guardianship) or *Imamah* (divine leadership), because not every Muslim believed in these concepts and may have resisted contemplating the argument if these terms were used. The tradition is known to mean those who believed in this matter (*wilayah*) and die while awaiting the final manifestation of it regardless of the period they live in.

The previous Imams, though present, were unable to lead and thus, even those who lived at that time and had conviction about *Imamah* are considered as having died while waiting for the Qaim—the Imam who was destined to lead the society—to come. This is evidenced by the famous *Dua Ahd,* taught by Imam Jafar al Sadiq, which is recited as a sign of loyalty to Imam Mahdi, indicating how intensely awaiting the Mahdi's rule was even in as early a period as that.

Anyone who was on the path of *Imamah* was waiting for it to manifest. The person asking the question from Imam Jafar al Sadiq was actually asking about when Imam al Sadiq would reach the fruition of his leadership and whether he would be alive to witness it. We must understand the significance of Imam al Sadiq's reference to being in the tent of the Qaim. In a camp, the leader is usually in one tent and then the commanders and soldiers are in other tents surrounding his. Being 'in' the tent of the Qaim refers to being part of his inner circle. The additional statement of being "like someone who was with the Messenger of God" further emphasizes the high status accorded to one who believes during the Imam's absence.

It becomes clear through these traditions that a believer should not worry about whether they are going to see the Imam or not. The important factor is having faith and waiting for *this matter* to be fulfilled. True *intidhar* is not about counting the days, it is about accepting the challenges of the present times and waiting with a fervent desire for change and a better spiritual existence.

Keeping Faith in the Mahdi During His Absence

To believe in Mahdi during his occultation is an instance of belief in the unseen (*imaan bil ghayb*). Some narrations have explicitly mentioned that as one instance of the verse of Surah al Baqarah:

الَّذِينَ يُؤْمِنُونَ بِالْغَيْبِ وَيُقِيمُونَ الصَّلَاةَ وَمِمَّا رَزَقْنَاهُمْ يُنْفِقُونَ ۞

Who believe in the Unseen, maintain the prayer and spend out of what We have provided for them. (2:3)

Mulla Fayz Kashani (d. 1050 AH), the famous Shia scholar, says in *Tafsir Safi* about this verse:

> They believe in whatever is hidden from their senses including the tawhid of God, the Prophethood of the Prophets, the rising of al Qaim, the raj'ah, resurrection, accounting, Paradise and Hell, and other issues in which they have to have faith but that cannot be seen and can be known only through the evidence placed by God.[107]

Fayz Kashani defines the unseen (*ghayb*) as being that which is believed in "through the evidence placed by God." In some narrations, one instance of the *ta'wil* (fulfilment) of this verse is given as having faith in the rising of the Qaim. For example, in *Kamalu al din* of Sheikh Saduq, Imam al Sadiq is quoted to have said, "*It is guidance for the God-wary; 'those who believe in the unseen' applies to those who acknowledge that the rising of the Qaim is Haqq.*"[108]

It is obvious that this is an application of the verse rather than its interpretation as we see in many other verses of the Qur'an. If that is the case, could not this expanded understanding of the unseen lead to superstition? After all, every faith is susceptible to superstition.

Fakhr al Din al Razi addresses this issue by saying that while it is possible that belief in the unseen may lead to superstition, it is important to distinguish between two types of belief in the unseen. The first is belief for which we have evidence and the second is belief for which we do not have any evidence. He argues that it is the first type of belief that is referred to in this verse. The verse commends the God-wary because they believe in an unseen for which there is religious evidence. This is because they reflect and use the evidence and then believe rather than relying on blind imitation or superstition.

Although belief in God entails belief in an absolutely unseen being, there is overwhelming evidence for His existence. Believing in God cannot, therefore, be categorized as a superstition; it is a belief based on evidence and logic, just like many things in various fields of science. Faith in the Prophet's connection to the higher realm is another example of such a belief. If someone claims that he has dreams or hears voices, believing him without evidence can be called superstition, but if someone claims a connection to God and then provides consistent, conclusive proof of this connection, believing in such a person is considered rational.

Faith in the twelfth Imam and his occultation is based on abundant evidence. Some of this evidence is observable and some of it comes from historical evidence such as the words of the infallible Prophet and Imams. However, superstition can be created around the belief in God, the Imam and the occultation; so when people claim to have spoken to Imam Mahdi telling them to pass on a message to others or things of similar nature, these can certainly be considered superstitions, since they cannot be established by verifiable evidence.

Imam al Baqir has said,

> A time will pass on people in which their Imam hides from them. How blessed are those who are steadfast in our affair during those times! The least reward for them is that the Creator will call them, 'O My servants! You believed in My secret and acknowledged My ghayb, so rejoice with the excellence of reward from Me'. [109]

The Merits of Expectation (*intidhar*)

A companion of Imam al Sadiq, Ammar ibn Musa, asked him about the period of expectation: "*I said to al Sadiq, 'Is worshipping God with an Imam from among you who is concealed in secret during the reign of batil better or worshipping God with a manifest Imam from among you when the haqq rules and is manifest?*"[110]

Before we look at Imam al Sadiq's response, we should recall that the Muslims viewed Imam al Sadiq in different ways: the Sunnis did not recognise him as an Imam, but they did respect him as a very pious and knowledgeable man from the family of the Prophet. Only his close companions recognised his true position as an Imam in the way we do today. He never publicly claimed *Imamah* or any status of leadership among Muslims as the authorities would have certainly killed him and persecuted his followers; this is why his *Imamah* remained concealed for the majority of Muslims. Imam al Baqir, Imam al Sadiq and the preceding Imams all concealed their true status because of the prevailing political environment.

This is the context behind Ibn Musa's questions about the status of 'worshipping with you' (Imam al Sadiq) who was concealed in secret during the reign of *batil* (oppression) or worshipping with a manifest Imam when the truth rules (at the time of the twelfth imam). Imam al Sadiq replied,

> O Ammar! By God, charity in secret is better than manifest charity. In the same manner, your worship in secret with your concealed Imam during the reign of batil is better... the worship with fear during the reign of batil is not like the worship with security during the reign of haqq.[111]

Of course, better here does not mean better in its actual reality; it means better in reward just as the charity given in secret is better in reward than the charity that is announced.

There are three possible eras of observance for the faithful: in the first era the Imam is visibly present, but his position is concealed; the second—which we are living in now—is when the Imam is in deeper concealment and he is not even visible or accessible; the third era will be when Imam Mahdi makes a visible stand and the affairs of truth and falsehood become clearly distinct. Imam al Sadiq uses an interesting analogy from Qur'anic guidance about charity in his answer that is echoed in the verse:

إِنْ تُبْدُوا الصَّدَقَاتِ فَنِعِمَّا هِيَ ۖ وَإِنْ تُخْفُوهَا وَتُؤْتُوهَا الْفُقَرَاءَ فَهُوَ خَيْرٌ لَكُمْ ۚ وَيُكَفِّرُ عَنْكُمْ مِنْ سَيِّئَاتِكُمْ ۗ وَاللَّهُ بِمَا تَعْمَلُونَ خَبِيرٌ ۞

If you disclose your charities, that is well, but if you hide them and give them to the poor, that is better for you, and it will atone for some of your misdeeds, and God is well aware of what you do. (2:271)

When performed in secret the action remains in its purest form, so while there are rewards for actions in both states, something done in secret or at a time of fear cannot be equated to something done publicly at a time of comfort and security.

During the *Imamah* of Imam al Sajjad and Imam al Kadhim, the Shia could not openly pray according to their creed because of the danger of imprisonment or death. Today, notwithstanding the persecution against the faithful in some parts of the world, Shias are generally free to practice openly according to their beliefs despite the Imam not being present with us. Given a choice, at which time would we prefer to live? To be at the time of Imam al Sadiq and practice faith with a pervading sense of fear or to be in the present where although Imam al Sadiq is not here, we can talk about Imam al Sadiq, follow his advice, extol his virtues and respond to anyone who insults him?

Having the security to worship as we please is a blessing that we must acknowledge and appreciate as a favour that not all Muslims enjoyed in the past. During the lives of the earlier Imams, the challenge was not only to practise the Shia creed under *taqiyyah* (dissimulation) but also to impart faith among the children and community in a way that ensures the continuity of the creed through generations. It was a very difficult set of circumstances, sometimes creating rifts and suspicions among family members in fear of government informers. In Iraq, during Saddam's reign, despite the Shia being in the majority, cousins feared each other and, in some cases, even husbands and wives lived in suspicion of each other. It was the same situation at the time of the Imams preceding the twelfth Imam. Their position of Imamate was secret and fraught with the dangers of consistent surveillance and persecution.

There are commonalities between the previous eras and the current time where even though the leadership was manifest, the Imam is in hiding to the extent that many Muslims have begun to challenge whether he really exists. There were periods preceding the twelfth Imam where believers faced greater hardships than we are facing today. When we look at what our brothers and sisters have endured, we cannot feel disheartened at not being able to communicate with the Imam. While people living earlier may have been at a material advantage, the rewards of maintaining belief and practising faith in these times will certainly be compensated and rewarded as being of a higher degree with regard to patience and perseverance.

In the earlier hadith, hearing the Imam's reply, Ibn Musa exclaimed: *"I said, 'May I be your ransom, if that is the case then we do not like to be from the companions of the Qaim in the days of haqq; because today under your Imamah and in your obedience, our acts count more than those living in the era of haqq.'"*[112]

This response shows how we can be limited in our understanding of matters from an individual, selfish perspective. The rewards of upholding one's faith in difficult times have a collective purpose and destiny that we often overlook when seeing things from our personal point of view. The Imam replied, *"Subhanallah! Do you not like God to manifest the truth and justice in cities? To improve the situation of human beings, to unify the faith, to reconcile between diverse hearts?"*[113]

Imam al Sadiq was himself waiting and preparing for the Qaim to come and establish these things because he did not have an open hand to do so. He continued,

> Do you not like that God is not disobeyed on earth, that the hudud of God are implemented on people, that the right is returned to its folks and they can manifest it and not hide any part of haqq out of fear from anyone of His creation? By God, O Ammar! Beware, not one of you would die in such circumstances which you are enduring unless they are higher in the eyes of God than the martyrs of Badr and Uhud. So rejoice![114]

This hadith shows that people have different duties at different times, and although the reward of their actions may be different, their altruistic aspiration must always have priority. While we strive and pray for his reappearance and the day when God's Word and Light will prevail, we should not be worried about whether we can talk or connect with Imam Mahdi nor should we insist on his coming to help us before the time is ripe. We must always view the *ghayba* as part of God's grand design and not as an individual or personal matter.

Patience with the plan and decrees of God and remaining steadfast on one's duties is paramount for a believer. The length of the absence of the Imam has been the greatest test for his followers and being patiently steadfast is of great importance. Impatience is a human flaw and one of the factors that has contributed to 27 people being recorded as having falsely claimed to be the Mahdi over the past 13 centuries. These false claimants acquired pockets of support amongst the Muslims because of people's frustrations with their situation and largely, because of a lack of proper recognition and understanding of who the personality of Imam Mahdi really is.[115]

The *Faraj* (Ease)

It is reported from Imam al Baqir that: "*The best worship is awaiting the ease (faraj).*"[116] The Arabic word used to refer to the arrival of the Mahdi is also *faraj*, as is stated in many narrations, which translates as 'ease'. Though *faraj* is a word that has different conceptual meanings in different narrations, in this context it denotes the open authority and compliance Imam Mahdi will have to administer society according to God's Decree.

The question we must ask ourselves is that given 'waiting' for the Mahdi has been accorded the status of worship, what does waiting mean? Can we count ourselves among those who 'wait' in the sense alluded to in the *hadith*?

What would be our attitude if our Imam were to reappear tomorrow? Would we be joyous, or would we panic because we are 'not ready'? Do we have to change anything to prepare ourselves to reach that state where we are ready to accept Imam at any moment? Waiting therefore cannot be understood to be an impassive state; it has to refer to an active attitude that reflects a sense of preparation.

Imam al Reza commenting on what Imam al Baqir meant by 'ease' said: "*Is not expecting the ease part of the ease? God, the Mighty, the High says, 'So wait; I too am waiting along with you.'*" [117]

The phrase "expecting the ease is part of the ease" means that if we are truly waiting for the mission and goals of Imam Mahdi to actualise including the establishment of justice, religiosity and all that has been promised, then it means that God has opened our hearts towards the light of guidance and therefore towards the ease. In such a case, it would not matter whether we experience the actual moment in our lifetimes; the ease would be with us because our hearts would have been guided towards it. This is one way in which the *faraj* can exist in our hearts.

Imam al Reza has further said:

> How nice is patience and waiting for the ease! Have you not heard the Word of God, 'So watch, I too am watching along with you' and His Word, 'So wait; I too am waiting along with you'? So, I advise you to patience, because the ease comes at the edge of disappointment; indeed those who were before you were more patient than you.[118]

This poignant advice from Imam al Reza on waiting with extreme patience and faith because the ease comes at the edge of disappointment prepares us for the fact that it will not come easily. This method of testing is not an exclusive concept to Imam Mahdi. Reflecting upon the Qur'an we can see many prophets who have faced high levels of difficulty, anguish, and disappointment with their respective communities before God's help for their ease was manifested.

حَتَّىٰ إِذَا اسْتَيْأَسَ الرُّسُلُ وَظَنُّوا أَنَّهُمْ قَدْ كُذِبُوا جَاءَهُمْ نَصْرُنَا فَنُجِّيَ مَن نَشَاءُ وَلَا يُرَدُّ بَأْسُنَا عَنِ الْقَوْمِ الْمُجْرِمِينَ ۞

When the apostles lost hope and [the people] thought that they had been told lies, Our Help came to them, and We delivered whomever We wished, and Our punishment will not be averted from the guilty lot. (12:110)

Before Prophet Musa, the Banu Israel spent hundreds of years under oppression and slavery. When Prophet Musa announced his apostleship and confronted Firaun, the oppression increased to the extent that the males of Banu Israel were killed and women left widowed and orphaned. The Holy Qur'an witnesses their complaints to Prophet Musa:

قَالُوا أُوذِينَا مِن قَبْلِ أَن تَأْتِيَنَا وَمِنْ بَعْدِ مَا جِئْتَنَا قَالَ عَسَىٰ رَبُّكُمْ أَن يُهْلِكَ عَدُوَّكُمْ وَيَسْتَخْلِفَكُمْ فِي الْأَرْضِ فَيَنظُرَ كَيْفَ تَعْمَلُونَ ۞

They said, "we were tormented before you came to us and [also] after you came to us." He said, "Maybe your Lord will destroy your enemy and make you successors in the land, and then He will see how you act." (7:129)

The effect of this extreme persecution was that only a small group from among the Banu Israel ended up believing in Prophet Musa; while everyone else rejected the faith. The fear of Firaun and the influence of the elite among the Banu Israel who had aligned with Firaun became so pervasive that no one was willing to endure the extreme hardship that belief in Prophet Musa entailed.

فَمَا آمَنَ لِمُوسَىٰ إِلَّا ذُرِّيَّةٌ مِّن قَوْمِهِ عَلَىٰ خَوْفٍ مِّن فِرْعَوْنَ وَمَلَئِهِمْ أَن يَفْتِنَهُمْ وَإِنَّ فِرْعَوْنَ لَعَالٍ فِي الْأَرْضِ وَإِنَّهُ لَمِنَ الْمُسْرِفِينَ ۞

But none believed in Moses except some youths from among his people, for the fear of Pharaoh and his elite that he would persecute them. For Pharaoh was indeed a tyrant in the land, and indeed he was an unrestrained [despot]. (10:83)

From the beginning of time, God in His infinite wisdom has decreed the law of placing ease at the edge of disappointment and hardship as the means to test the hearts of the believers. Those who fail in the middle receive their reward based on the level of faith they achieved. Those who transcend that threshold and cross over into deeper conviction are the ones who are taken to the closeness of God.

قَالَ مُوسَىٰ لِقَوْمِهِ اسْتَعِينُوا بِاللَّهِ وَاصْبِرُوا ۖ إِنَّ الْأَرْضَ لِلَّهِ يُورِثُهَا مَن يَشَاءُ مِنْ عِبَادِهِ ۖ وَالْعَاقِبَةُ لِلْمُتَّقِينَ ۞

Musa said to his people, 'Turn to God for help and be patient. The earth indeed belongs to God, and He gives its inheritance to whomever He wishes of His servants, and the outcome will be in favour of the God wary.' (7:128)

This is why Imam Ali also advised, "*Wait for the ease and do not be disappointed from the Mercy of God; indeed the act most loved by God is waiting for the ease.*" [119]

Imam al Sadiq has said, "*There is an era for us that God will bring whenever He wishes.*" Then he said, "*Whoever likes to be among the companions of the Qaim must wait and act righteously and with good akhlaq; he is the one who is truly waiting.*"[120]

Such remarks completely negate the misguided attitude that 'we need to wait for Imam Mahdi to come and sort everything out'. This is certainly not the waiting expected of us; it is just passing our time and escaping our responsibility—like so many other nations before have done.

In Preparation for His Coming

Many books of varying quality have been written about what preparation for the arrival of the Imam entails. Some contain as many as 60 to 70 points on how to prepare ourselves for his coming; some go so far as listing learning martial arts as an example of a way to prepare. While learning such an art is not without merit, these are not the kind of things that the Imam requires from his followers when he comes.

The foremost requirement is that our hearts should not reject him when he comes; this is vital. The Jews in Medina were waiting for centuries because clear prophecies existed in their literature about the last Prophet coming to the area around the mountains of Uhud. They were the ones who migrated and populated the areas of Yathrib before anyone else, in anticipation of his coming. Yet when he came, they were amongst the first to reject him.

وَلَمَّا جَاءَهُمْ كِتَابٌ مِنْ عِنْدِ اللَّهِ مُصَدِّقٌ لِمَا مَعَهُمْ وَكَانُوا مِنْ قَبْلُ يَسْتَفْتِحُونَ عَلَى الَّذِينَ كَفَرُوا فَلَمَّا جَاءَهُمْ مَا عَرَفُوا كَفَرُوا بِهِ فَلَعْنَةُ اللَّهِ عَلَى الْكَافِرِينَ ۞

And when there came to them a Book from God, confirming that which is with them—and earlier they would pray for victory over the pagans [through him]—so when there came to them what they recognized, they denied it. So may the curse of God be on the faithless! (2:89)

الَّذِينَ آتَيْنَاهُمُ الْكِتَابَ يَعْرِفُونَهُ كَمَا يَعْرِفُونَ أَبْنَاءَهُمْ وَإِنَّ فَرِيقًا مِنْهُمْ لَيَكْتُمُونَ الْحَقَّ وَهُمْ يَعْلَمُونَ ۞

Those whom We have given the Book recognize him just as they recognize their sons, but a part of them indeed conceal the truth while they know (2:146)

The reason they rejected the Prophet when he arrived was that he was not as they expected him to be; the things he said did not resonate with their prevailing ideas and values. Over the centuries, their faith had become dependent on the teachings of errant rabbis who convinced them otherwise, using several fallacious arguments such as 'if he says or does this or that believe him, otherwise do not'. Many rejected the Prophet for the sole reason that he was an *ummi*—a Gentile—though the scriptures with the rabbis said otherwise.

Another clear example from history is the great tragedy of Karbala. The people of Kufa persistently, in their thousands, asked Imam Husayn to come and lead them against the oppression of Banu Umayyah. Yet we all know the outcome; thousands joined the army of Yazid leaving Imam Husayn alone.

The question we need to ask ourselves is: did the people of Kufa intentionally deceive Imam Husayn? We know this was not the case; they sincerely longed for him to be in their midst. The problem was that when external pressures fell upon them, their hearts could not withstand this test and they deserted Imam Husayn despite being fully aware of his status and of their own continuous persecution at the hands of the Ummayads.

If we want to succeed in our *intidhar* and avoid the mistakes of our predecessors, we must learn from the history. We must seriously consider the qualities that made some believers stand firm on faith and caused others to fall into error and betrayal. We must then honestly apply these standards to ourselves and assess our own state of belief.

We have to think about how we may react if Imam Mahdi arrives and says things that do not resonate with our hearts. He may ask us to obey him in matters that we would find difficult to accept or endure. We would not be able to hide or modulate our reaction and this would be a test to bring forth whatever our character has been up to that point. The human heart can easily become rebellious in many aspects, especially if we do not focus on matters of faith and leave our hearts to become unresponsive; in this case, would run a real risk of (God forbid!) rejecting the Imam.

It is critical as individuals and a community, to prepare for his arrival in such a way that we train our hearts and minds to be in line with what he is going to bring. This requires continuous reflection and striving to change for the better if we are sincere.

Developing and guarding *taqwa* (mindfulness of God) during this period of waiting is of utmost importance. *Taqwa* is not a station to achieve but a critical provision for our journey towards God. Fulfilling obligatory acts and staying away from what is prohibited is only a basic pre-condition. There are countless examples in our lives, and in history, of people who have fallen from a high station because they were somehow deceived into believing that they were safe from the vagaries of the soul and the deceptions of Shaytan.

The best way to nurture this *taqwa* is to foster a healthy relationship with the Qur'an. Many traditions have stated that Imam Mahdi will establish the Qur'an when he comes. Although many Muslims recite the Qur'an and some have even memorised it, our understanding of this holy text is very superficial. The more we try to understand the Qur'an, the more we will be guided as our thoughts and beliefs will increasingly converge with the concepts of the Qur'an.

Concerning how the Mahdi will establish the Qur'an, Imam Ali is reported to have said, "*He will bring back all opinions to the Qur'an after they have made the Qur'an subservient to opinions.*"[121] It is true that in our current situation, the Qur'an has already become subservient to people's opinions. Different schools of theology and law have interpreted the Qur'an according to their own opinions. Many even among the same denomination have different understandings of the Qur'an. This is the case because we read the Qur'an superficially and adapt its meanings to suit our opinions. Some Jews made a similar mistake, and this became one of the factors in their rejection of Prophet Muhammad:

$$\text{وَمِنْهُمْ أُمِّيُّونَ لَا يَعْلَمُونَ الْكِتَابَ إِلَّا أَمَانِيَّ وَإِنْ هُمْ إِلَّا يَظُنُّونَ}$$

And among them are the illiterate who know nothing of the Book except hearsay, and they only make conjectures. (2:78)

We certainly do not wish to be of those about whom the Prophet shall say on Judgement Day:

$$\text{وَقَالَ الرَّسُولُ يَا رَبِّ إِنَّ قَوْمِي اتَّخَذُوا هَٰذَا الْقُرْآنَ مَهْجُورًا}$$

And the Apostle will say, 'O my Lord! Indeed, my people consigned this Qur'an to oblivion.' (25:30)

Imam Mahdi will bring us all back to the true understanding and interpretation of the Qur'an. However, in the present time as well, the deeper we strive to understand the Qur'an, the easier God will make it for our hearts to accept what the Imam says when he comes.

The *duas* taught by the Imams are also powerful tools to improve our God-consciousness and spiritual position. These blessed words of the truthful ones (*siddiqun*) have a deep impact on the hearts that goes beyond the actual words. As Imam Ali said, *"He will take desires back to guidance after they have made guidance subservient to their desires."* The more we practise faith, the more we do good and support what is just *(amr bil ma'roof)*, the more we can absorb guidance and it establishes its strong roots in our hearts. Therefore, when Imam Mahdi comes our hearts will be ready for him. All other aspects of preparation are superficial compared to the preparation of the heart in a way that we do not falter or somehow feel alien to the guidance Imam Mahdi brings.

Additionally, it is important to continuously cultivate and maintain a strong spirit of resistance against falsehood, oppression, and injustices, both in our hearts and through our actions. This resistance and active opposition to whatever is false *(nahiya anil munkir)* is a necessary condition to continue our movement towards the light of God.

$$\text{فَمَنْ يَكْفُرْ بِالطَّاغُوتِ وَيُؤْمِنْ بِاللَّهِ فَقَدِ اسْتَمْسَكَ بِالْعُرْوَةِ الْوُثْقَىٰ لَا انْفِصَامَ لَهَا ۗ وَاللَّهُ سَمِيعٌ عَلِيمٌ}$$

So one who disavows the Rebels and has faith in Allah has held fast to the firmest handle for which there is no breaking; and Allah is all-hearing, all-knowing. (2:256)

Imam al Sadiq's hadith mentioned earlier further underlines this point: *"There is an era for us that God will bring it whenever he wishes."* Then he said, *"Whoever likes to be among the companions of al Qaim must wait and act righteously and with good conduct* [akhlaq]; *and he is the one who is truly waiting."*[122]

Continuously striving towards unity, justice, fraternity, morality, selflessness and other important communal aspects of active waiting have great bearing on preparedness for the arrival of the Mahdi.

Endnotes

1. This theme in spirit, remains present in both the Old and New Testaments. It is also visible in non-canonical books like Book of Enoch. Examples of the recurring theme are:

- Psalms 37:9, NIV: For those who are evil will be destroyed, but those who hope in the LORD will inherit the land.

- Psalms 37:22 NIV: those the LORD blesses will inherit the land, but those he curses will be destroyed.

- Psalms 37:28-29: For the LORD loves the just and will not forsake his faithful ones. Wrongdoers will be completely destroyed; the offspring of the wicked will perish. The righteous will inherit the land and dwell in it forever.

- Enoch 5:7 For the chosen; there will be light, joy, and peace, and they will inherit the earth. But for you, the impious, there will be a curse.

2. In *Muntakhib al-Athar fi al-Imam al-Ithnaa Ashar* – Ayatoullah Safi Golpaygani has collected a total of 6036 hadith about Imam Mahdi including 560 from the Holy Prophet

3. Apart from a very small minority like Ismaili Muslims

4. These were, al-Sheikh Ibn Hajar al-Haithami al-Shafi'i, al-Sheikh Ahmad b. Abi al-Sarwar b. Saba al-Hanafi, al-Sheikh Muhammad b. Muhammad al-Khattaabi al-Maliki, and al-Sheikh Yahya b. Muhammad al-Hanbali,

5. According to Kourani (*Asr al-Zuhur*), manuscripts of this book are available in libraries in Haidar Abad and Damascus, and since 1924 the book has also been available in the library of British Museum.

6. In *Mahdiy-e Ahl al-Bayt*, Dhabihullah Mahallati lists 40 books by Sunni scholars and 110 books by Shia scholars written exclusively on the Mahdi. Khusro Qasim of Aligarh University, in his book *Imam Mahdi son of Imam Hasan Al-Askari-In view of Sunni Scholars* lists 32 books exclusively written on the subject of Imam Mahdi by Sunni scholars and 144 books of Sunni scholars that discuss traditions and verses related to Imam Mahdi.
Suhaib Hasan in his book T*he Concept of the Mahdi among Ahl-Sunna* lists 67 Sunni high ranking traditionists and scholars who wrote in support of the idea of the Mahdi.

7. Majlisi, *Bihar al-anwar* (Beirut: Mu'sassat al-Wafa', n.d.), vol. 25. P, 289.

8. Kulayni, *Al-Kafi*, (Tehran, Dar al-Kutub al-Islamiyyah, 1388 sh.), vol. 1 p, 179.

9. Sharif Razi, *Nahjul Balagha*, [al-islam.org], Sayings and Letters, Hadith 147, page 449

10. Sharif Razi, *Nahjul Balagha*, [al-islam.org], Sayings and Letters, Hadith 432, page 614

11. Fakhr Al Din Razi, *Tafsir Kabir*, (Beirut: Daru Ihyai' Turath al-Arabi, 1420 A.H.), volume 14, p. 192

12. See *Mafatih Al Jinan* for Ziyarah al Jami'ah al Kabirah

13. Baqir Sharif Al-Quraysh, *The Life of Imam Jafar al Sadiq*, (Translated by Majid Asadi, Qum: Ansariyan Publications n.d.), p 323.

14. Baqir Sharif Al-Quraysh, *The Life of Imam Jafar al Sadiq*, (Translated by Majid Asadi, Qum: Ansariyan Publications, n.d.), page 234

15 Majlisi, *Bihar al-anwar* (Beirut: Mu'sassat al-Wafa', n.d.), Vol 89, page 79

16. Ibid

17. Suyuti, *al Durr al Manthour*, (Qum: Aytollah Mar'ashi Library, 1404 A.H.), volume 4, page 45 quoting from *Tafsir al Tabari*

18. Al Hakim al Nayshaburi, *al-Mustadral 'ala Sahihayn*, (Beirut: Dar al-Kutub al 'Ilmiyyah, 1990), vol. 3, p. 129.

19. Tha'labi, *Al-Kashf wa-l-bayān'an fi tafsīr al-Qur'an*, (Beirut: Daru Ihyai' Turath al-Arabi, 1422 A.H.),), vol. 5, p. 272.

20. Kulayni, *Al- Kafi*, (English edition, translated by Muhammad Sarwar and Published by Islamic Seminary INCNY, 1999) Ch. 10, hadith 485, in-chapter hadith 4,

21. Ibid

22. Kulayni, *Al-Kafi*, (English edition, translated by Muhammad Sarwar and Published by Islamic Seminary INCNY, 1999) Ch. 10, hadith 482, in-chapter hadith 1,

23. Majlisi, *Bihar al-anwar* (Beirut: Mu'sassat al-Wafa', n.d.), vol. 2, p22.,

24. *Ijtiba'* and *Istifa* are both terms used in the Qur'an to denote Divine selection. While similar in meaning they have exoteric and esoteric components of differentiation, beyond the scope of this book.

25. Kulayni, *Al- Kafi*, (English edition, Translated by Muhammad Sarwar and Published by Islamic Seminary INCNY, 1999), Ch. 6, hadith 443, in-chapter hadith 3.

26. Kulayni, *Al- Kafi*, (English edition, translated by Muhammad Sarwar and Published by Islamic Seminary INCNY, 1999), Ch. 6, hadith 442, in-chapter hadith 2.
Interestingly there are Hadith in *Sahih Muslim* and *Bukhari* alluding to the same concept in a slightly altered wording. In *Sahih Muslim* Kitab Al Imara for example Hadith 4476 from Abdullah ibn Umar narrates: *It has been narrated on the authority of 'Abdullah that the Messenger of God (may peace be upon him) said: The Caliphate will remain among the Quraish even if only two persons are left (on the earth).*
A similarly worded hadith also from Abdullah Ibn Umar is narrated in *Sahih Bukhari* in Book 61 on the Virtues of the Quraysh, Hadith 11: *Authority of ruling will remain with Quraysh, even if only two of them remained.*

27. Sharif al Razi, *Nahjul Balagha*, Letters and Sayings, [al Islam.org], Hadith 147, page 447.

28. *Mafatih al Jinan*, Ziyaraht al Warith

29. Sharif al Razi, *Nahjul al Balagha*, [al-Islam.org], Hadith 147, page 449

30. Ibid

31. Kulayni, Al Kafi, (English edition, translated by Muhammad Sarwar and Published by Islamic Seminary INCNY, 1999), ch. 1, hadith 428.

32. Ayatollah Lutfullah Gulpaygani, Fatimmiyah is Ashura, Sermon of Fadak, Lady Fatima Zahra, cited from al-Ihtijaj of Shaykh al-Tabarsi by Ayatullah Lutfullah Gulpaygani in his book 'Fatimmiyah is Ashura, translated by Saleem Bhimji – source: al-islam.org

33. Kulayni, *Al-Kafi* (Tehran, Dar al Kutub al Islamiyyah, 1388 sh.), Volume 1 - Page 177

34 Majlisi, *Bihar al-anwar* (Beirut: Mu'sassat al-Wafa', n.d.), vol. 7, p.279.

35. Al-Khazzaz, Ali ibn Mohammad, *Kifayt al-athar fi al-nass 'ala al-a'immat al-ithna 'ashar,* (Noor Digital Library), pp. 24-25.

36. Muslim ibn Hajjaj, *Sahih Muslim*, Kitab al Imarah, Book 20, Number 4478

37. Bukhari, Mohammad ibn Isma'il, *Sahih al-Bukhari*, Kitabul Ahkam, Book 89 Hadith 329.

38. Muslim ibn Hajjaj, *Sahih Muslim*, Kitab al Imarah, Book 20, Number 4480

39. Other Ahl Sunnah sources for the hadith of twelve khalifas include Bukhari, *Sahih al-Bukhari*, vol. 8, p. 127, Muslim, *Sahih Muslim*, vol. 3, hadith 1453, Abū Dāwūd, Sunan, vol. 4, p. 106, Tirmidhi, *Sunan al-Tirmidhi*, vol. 4, p. 501, Ahmad b. Hanbal, *Musnad*, vol. 1, p. 406, Ahmad b. Hanbal, *Musnad*, vol. 6, p. 222., Suyuti, *Tarikh al-khulafah*, p. 210, uyuti, *Tarikh al-khulafah*, p. 10-12., Ibn Hajar, Fath al-bārī, vol. 13, p. 214., Qunduzi, *Yanabi' al-mawadda*, vol. 2, p. 535. Abu 'Abd Allah Ahmad b. Hanbal al-Shaybani, *Musnad* (Cairo: Muasassat Qurtubah) [annotator: Shu'ayb al-Arnaut], vol. 5, p. 96, # 20944, Abu al-Husayn Muslim b. al-Hajjaj al-Qushayri al-Naysaburi, *Sahih Muslim* (Beirut: Dar Ihya al-Turath al-'Arabi) [annotator: Muhammad Fuad 'Abd al-Baqi], vol. 3, p. 1453, # 1822, Abu 'Abd Allah Ahmad b. Hanbal al-Shaybani, *Musnad* (Cairo: Muasassat Qurtubah) [annotator: Shu'ayb al-Arnaut], vol. 5, p. 106, # 21051

40. Bukhari, Mohammad ibn Isma'il, *Sahih al-Bukhari*, Hadith 3667 and 3668, Book 62 Hadith 19 (wordings are similar but not exact)

41. Ahmad ibn Hanbal, *Musnad* (Cairo: Muasassat Qurtubah) [annotated by Shu'ayb al-Arnaut], vol. 5, p. 106.

42. Abu Dawud, Tirmidhi, Ahmad ibn Hanbal, Abu Yula, Hakim, Suyuti, Tabarani, Darqatni, Abu Nu-aym, Khatib and Ibn Asakir and many others have accepted the fact of the ultimate rule of Imam Mahdi, who is the last of the twelve successors of the Holy Prophet from among his Ahlul Bayt. This has also been verified as Sahih by Sheikh Albani in his annotation of the hadith quoted by Abu Bakr b. Abi 'Asim, Ahmad b. 'Amr b. al-Dhahhak b. Mukhlid al-Shaybani, *Kitab al-Sunnah* (al-Maktab al-Islami; 1st edition, 1400 A. H.) [annotator: Muhammad Nasir al-Din al-Albani], vol. 2, p. 527, # 1109

43. Abu Bakr Ibn al-'Arabi, *'Aridat al Ahwadhi bi Sharh Sahihunan al Tirmidhi*, (Beirut, Dar al Kutub al 'ilmiyyah, 1997) vol. 9, pp.:68-69

44. Al-Suyuti, *Tarikh al-Khulafa*, (Beirut, Dar Sadir, 1997

45. Muhiyuddin Ibn-al- Arabi, *al Futuhat al -Makkiyah*, (Beirut, Dar Sadir, n.d.), Ch.apter 366

46. Al-Saffar, Mohammad ibn al Hasan, *Basa'r al Darjat*, (Qum: Ayatollah Mar'ashi Library, 1404 A.H.), p.340

47. Kulayni, *Al-Kafi*, (English edition, Translated by Muhammad Sarwar and Published by Islamic Seminary INCNY, 1999) ch. 3, hadith 421-423, in-chapter hadith 1-3.

48. Tafsir MM Pooya and Mir Ahmed Ali provides some background to this verse is that:

> 'Some pagans and hypocrites planned secretly to recite words praising idolatry alongside the recitation of the Holy Prophet, while he was praying, in such a way that the people would think as if they were recited by him. Once when the Holy Prophet was reciting verses 19 and 20 of Najm, one of the pagans recited: "Tilkal gharani-al ula wa inna shafa-atahuma laturja" (These are the lofty (idols), verily their intercession is sought after) As soon as this was recited, the conspirators shouted in delight to make the people believe that it was the Holy Prophet who said these words. Here, the Qur'an is stating the general pattern the enemies of God followed when they were convinced that the people were paying attention to the teachings of the messengers of God and sincerely believing in them. They would mix their false doctrines with the original teachings so as to make the Divine message a bundle of contradictions. This kind of satanic insertions are referred to in this verse, and supported by Ha Mim: 26. It is sheer blasphemy to say that satanic forces can influence the messengers of God. The Quran has repeatedly asserted that Satan shall have no authority whatsoever over the purified servants of God. Please refer to the commentary of Ibrahim: 22 and Nahl: 99 and 100 according to which Satan has no authority over the purified servants of God.'

49. Kulayni, *Al Kafi*. (English edition, translated by Muhammad Sarwar and Published by Islamic Seminary INCNY, 1999), Ch. 3, hadith 421, in-chapter h 1,

50. Kulayni, *Al-Kafi*, (Tehran, Dar al-Kutub al-Islamiyyah, 1388 sh.), vol. 1, p. 393.

51. Kulayni, *Al-Kafi*, (English edition, translated by Muhammad Sarwar

and Published by Islamic Seminary INCNY, 1999) Ch. 53, hadith 705, in-chapter hadith 4,

52. Muslim ibn Hajjaj, *Sahih Muslim*, (Sunnah.com), hadith 2398a, book 44, hadith 34.

53. Bukhari, Mohammad ibn Isma'il, *Sahih al-Bukhari*, vol. 5, hadith 3689; Muslim ibn Hajjaj, Sahih Muslim, vol. 7, P. 115

54. Al-Manawi, Zayn al din Mohammad, *Fayd al-Qadir* (Cairo: al Maktab al Tijariyyah al Kubra, 13576 A.H.), vol. 4, p. 664

55. Al Hakim al Nayshaburi, *al-Mustadrak 'ala Sahihayn*, (Beirut: Dar al-Kutub al 'Ilmiyyah, 1990), vol. 3, p. 109, Ahmad ibn Hanbal, *Musnad* (Cairo: Muasassat Qurtubah) [annotated by Shu'ayb al-Arnaut],vol. 5, p. 181.

56. Ahl-Sunnah references include: Ahmad bin Muhammad bin Hanbal, *Musnad* (Egypt: 131 H) pages 259, 285, 292; Muslim bin Hajjaj Nayshapuri, *Sahih Muslim* (Egypt: 1349) vol. 4, page 116; Abi Isa Muhammad Tirmidhi, *Sahih Tirmidhi* (Sharah ibnul Arabi) (Egypt: 1352 H) vol. 13 pages 200, 248; Ahmed ibn Shu-ayb Nisa-i, *Khasa-is* (Egypt: 1348 H) page 4; Ibn Jarir Tabari, *Tafsir Tabari* (Jama ul Bayan fi Tafsir il Quran) (Egypt: 1331 H) vol.22, page 5; Sulayman bin Ahmad Al Tibrani, *Al Mu-jam Al Saghir* (Dehli: 1311 H), page 34, 75; Hakim Nayshapuri, *Al Mustadrak* (Hyderabad Deccan: 1334 H), pages 146, 147, 148; Yusuf bin Abdullah ibni Abdul Birr, *Al Isti-ab* (Hyderabad Deccan: 1346 H), vol. 2, page 460; Ali bin Ahmad Al Wahidi, *Asbab ul Nuzul* (Egypt: 1315 H) pages 266, 267.

Ibn-Kathir and Maudoodi have also narrated this in all versions of their respective tafsirs of this verse (33:33) - among many other Ahl Sunnah exegetes.

A hadith has also been reported that for six months after the incident of the cloak, the Prophet used to pass every day at Fajr prayers outside the door of Lady Fatima saying: *As-Salat O People of the house! Allah only wishes to remove the Rijs from you, O members of the family, and to purify you with thorough purification.* Tirmidhi, Jamia Tirmidhi (sunnah.com), Hadith 3206, In book reference Book 47, Hadith 258

57. Tirmidhi, *Jamia Tirmidhi* [sunnah.com], Hadith 3205, In book reference Book 47, Hadith 257; Tirmidhi, *Jamia Tirmidhi* (sunnah.com) Hadith 3787 and 3871, In book reference Book 49, Hadith 186 and 271

58. Muslim ibn Hajjaj, *Sahih Muslim*, [Sunnah.com], Hadith 2424, In-book reference Book 44, Hadith 91

59. Al Hakim al Nayshaburi, *al-Mustadrak 'ala Sahihayn*, (Beirut: Dar al-Kutub al 'Ilmiyyah, 1990) Al-Hakim al-Nayshapuri, vol. 2, p. 343, and vol. 3, p. 150

60. Sharif al-Razi, *Nahj al-Balaghah*, sermon 190

61. Ayatoullah Safi Golpaygani, *Selected Narrations about the 12th Imam*, Volume 2, [https://www.al-islam.org/selected-narrations-about-twelfth-imam-volume-2-lutfullah-safi-golpaygani]

62. Saduq, Mohammad ibn Ali, *Kamal al din wa Tamamu al Ni' mah*, (Tehran: Dar al Kutub al Islamiyyah, 1395 A.H.), vol. 1, p. 262

63. In his detailed research, Imam Mahdi in View of Sunni Scholars, Khusro Qasim has listed 40 Sunni scholars of prominence who have affirmed that Imam Mahdi is indeed the son of Imam Hasan al Askari and have also confirmed the preceding chain of Imams. We have also in earlier chapters quoted the belief of the famous Sufi mystic Ibn-Arabi in all 12 Imams.

64. Al-Qunduzi, Solayman ibn Ibrahim, *Yanabi' al-Mawaddah*, (Najaf: Maktabah al-Haydariyah, 1411 A.H.) , p. 590.

65. Saduq, Mohammad ibn Ali, *Kamal al din wa Tamamu al Ni' mah*, (Tehran: Dar al Kutub al Islamiyyah, 1395 A.H.) vol. 2, pp. 372–373, al-Khazzaz, Ali ibn Mohammad, *Kifayt al-athar fi al-nass 'ala al-a'immat al-ithna 'ashar*, (Noor Digital Library), pp. 275–277, al-Qunduzi, Solayman ibn Ibrahim, *Yanabi' al-Mawaddah*, (Najaf: Maktabah al-Haydariyah, 1411 A.H.), p. 454.

66. Ibid

67. Ayatoullah Safi Golpaygani, *Selected Narrations about the 12th Imam*, Volume 2, (https://www.al-islam.org/selected-narrations-about-twelfth-imam-volume-2-lutfullah-safi-golpaygani), cited from Suduq, Ikmaluddin

68. Majlisi, *Bihar al-anwar* (Beirut: Mu'sassat al-Wafa', n.d.), volume 1, p. 439 citing Ikmaluddin of Suduq

69. Fadl ibn Shadhan, Abu Muhammad, *Mukhtasaru lthbati'r-Raj'ah* (al-islam.org, translated by Syed Saeed Akhtar Rizvi).

70. Kulayni, *Al-Kafi*, (Tehran, Dar al-Kutub al-Islamiyyah, 1388 sh.), vol. 1, p. 340.

71. Kulayni, *Al Kafi*, (English edition, translated by Muhammad Sarwar and Published by Islamic Seminary INCNY, 1999), Ch. 80, hadith 906, in-chapter hadith 19.

72. Al-Nu'mani, Mohammad ibn Ibrahim, *al Ghayba*, (Tehran, Nashr-e Saduq, 1397 A.H.) pp. 171-172

73. Kulayni, *Al-Kafi*, (Tehran, Dar al-Kutub al-Islamiyyah, 1388 sh.), vol. 1, p. 337-338

74. Saduq, Mohammad ibn Ali, *Kamal al din wa Tamamu al Ni' mah*, (Tehran: Dar al Kutub al Islamiyyah, 1395 A.H.) Saduq, Ikamalaldin: Part 2, p. 481-482

75. Majlisi, *Bihar al-anwar* (Beirut: Mu'sassat al-Wafa', n.d.), vol. 52, p. 328

76. Ibid, vol 52, p. 391

77. Ibid, vol 52, p. 321.

78. Sharif Razi, *Nahjul Balaghah* , Sermons, Sermon 138

79. Ibid

80. Majlisi, *Bihar al-anwar*, (Beirut: Mu'sassat al-Wafa', n.d.), vol. 77, p. 300

81. Ibid, vol 2, page 285

82. Ibid, vol. 51, p. 78.

83. Ibid, vol 52, p. 81.

84. Ibid, vol. 52, p. 362.

85. Ayatollah Safi Golpaygani, *Selected Narrations about the 12th Imam* [https://www.al-islam.org/selected-narrations-about-twelfth-imam-volume-2-lutfullah-safi-golpaygani], volume 2, hadith 640 cited from *Kitabu Fadl ibn Shadhan*

86. A measure of weight equal to 750 grams.

87. Ayatollah Safi Golpaygani, *Muntakhab al-Athar fi al Imam al-Thani Ashar*, (Tehran: Maktabat Al Sadr, n.d.), p.74.

88. Majlisi, *Bihar al-anwar*, (Beirut: Mu'sassat al-Wafa', n.d.), vol. 51, p 83

89. Al-Nu'mani, Mohammad ibn Ibrahim, *al Ghayba*, (Tehran, Nashr-e Saduq, 1397 A.H.), p 22.

90. Ibn Tawus, *Al Malahim wa al fitan fi Zuhuri Gha'ib al Mutazar*, (Qum: Manshourat al-Razi, 1978), p. 165

91. Al- Mufid, Mohammad ibn Mohammad ibn Nu'man, *Al Irshad,* (Beirut, Dar al-Mufid, 1993), vol. 2 p. 384

92. Majlisi, *Bihar al-anwar,* (Beirut: Mu'sassat al-Wafa', n.d.), vol. 52, p. 337.

93. Ibid, vol. 10, p. 78

94. Ibid, vol. 52, p. 338.

95. Saduq, Mohammad ibn Ali, *Kamal al din wa Tamamu al Ni' mah*, (Tehran: Dar al Kutub al Islamiyyah, 1395 A.H.), p 703.

96. Majlisi, *Bihar al-anwar* (Beirut: Mu'sassat al-Wafa', n.d.), vol. 52, p. 352

97. Ibid, vol. 52 , p 336.

98. Sharif Razi, *Nahjul Balaghah*, sermon 149.

99. Majlisi, *Bihar al-anwar* (Beirut: Mu'sassat al-Wafa', n.d.), vol. 53 ,pp 43

100. Ahmad ibn Hanbal, *Musnad* (Cairo: Muasassat Qurtubah, n. d.), Hadith 23814

101. Majlisi, *Bihar al-anwar,* (Beirut: Mu'sassat al-Wafa', n.d.), vol. 52, p. 316

102. Ibid, vol 52 p. 384

103. Al-Khoi, Mirza Habibullah, *Minhaj al Bara'ah*, (Qum: Bonyad-e Farhangi Imam Mahdi, 1405 A.H.), vol. 8, p. 353

104. Majlisi, *Bihar al-anwar,* (Beirut: Mu'sassat al-Wafa', n.d.), vol. 53, p. 62

105. Ibid, vol. 52, p. 125.

106. Ibid, vol. 52 , p 126

107. Fayz Kashani, Mulla Mohsin, *Tafsir al Safi*, (Tehran: Sadra, 1415 A.H.), volume 1 , page 92.

108. Saduq, Mohammad ibn Ali, *Kamal al din wa Tamamu al Ni' mah*, (Tehran: Dar al Kutub al Islamiyyah, 1395 A.H.), p. 46

109. Saduq, Mohammad ibn Ali, *Kamal al din wa Tamamu al Ni' mah*, (Tehran: Dar al Kutub al Islamiyyah, 1395 A.H.), p. 330

110. Kulayni, *Al-Kafi*, (Tehran, Dar al-Kutub al-Islamiyyah, 1388 sh.), vol. 1 p. 334

111. Ibid

112. Ibid

113. Ibid

114. Ibid

115. Suhaib Hasan in his book *The Mahdi Among the Ahl Sunnah* lists the people through history who have claimed to be Mahdi

1) Salih B Tarif Al-Barghawati (D.174AH/789CE), North Africa
2) Muhammad B. Abdullah B. Hasan B. Hasan B Ali. (D.145AH/762CE), Medina
3) Abdullah B. Maimun Al Ahwazi, Eastern Arabia/Iran (D.200AH/815CE)
4) Ahmad B. Kayyal Al Balkhi
5) Hamdan B.Ash'ath Al Qirmiti (Circa 270AH/883CE), Kufa
6) Yahya Bin Zakrawaih Al Qirmiti (D.290AH/902CE), Syria
7) Husain B.Zakrawaih (D.291AH/903AH), Damascus
8) Abu Sa'id Al Junabi Al Qirmiti (D.301AH/913CE), Qatif, Eastern Arabis
9) Ubaidullah Al-Mahdi (D.322AH/933CE), Nasirun (Al-Maghreb)
10) Muhammad B. Abdullah Tumart Al-Hasani (D.524AH/1129CE), Sus (Al-Maghreb)
11) Mahmud Wahid Gilani (Appeared in 600AH/1203CE), Gilan (Iran)
12) Ahmad B. Abdullah Al-Mulatham (D.740AH/1339/CE), Egypt, recanted his claim in later life after imprisonment
13) Abd al Aziz Al-Tarabulusi (appeared 717AH/1317CE), Tripoli Libya
14) Uwais Rumi (appeared around 900AH/1500CE), Turkey, later recanted his claim
15) Sayid Muhammad Jaunpuri 847AH/11443-910AH/1504, India
16) Jalal Ud Din Akbar (D.1014AH/1605CE), Mughal Emperor, India
17) Abul Abbas Ahmad B. Abdullah Al- Sajalmasi (D.1022AG/1613CE), Marrakesh
18) Syed Muhammad Nur Baksh Jaunpuri (D.before 1040AH/1630CE)
19) Ahmad B.Ali Al Muhairathi (1050AH/1640CE)
20) Muhammad Al-Mahdi Al Azmaki (D. after 1070AH/1659CE)

Kurdistan

21) Muhammad B. Abdullah Al Kurdi (circa. 1075AH/1664CE), Mosul. He later recanted after imprisonment. Interestingly around the same time in Turkey, a Spanish Jew Sabatai Sevi, also claimed to be the Messiah and thousands of Jews from all over the world joined him. He was also defeated and imprisoned by the Ottomans.

22) Mirza Ali Muhammad Bab (D.1266AH/1850CE), Shiraz Iran. He was the precursor to development of the Bahai faith

23) Muhammad Ahmad Al Mahdi Al-Sudani (D.1303AH/1885), Sudan

24) Mirza Ghulam Ahmad Qadian (D.1326AH/1908CE), India. He is the founder of the Qadiani/Ahmadiyya sect with the majority believing he was a Nabi and the Promised Messiah and one group within believing him to be the Promised Mahdi.

25) Muhammad B. Abdullah Hasan Al-Sumali (D.1340AH/1921CE), Somalia

26) Yahya Ainullah Bihari (D.around 1349AH/1930), Bihar, India

27) Muhammad B. Abdullah Al-Qahtani, (D.1400AH/1979), Mecca

116. Majlisi, *Bihar al-anwar*, (Beirut: Mu'sassat al-Wafa', n.d.), vol. 52, p. 125

117. Ibid, vol. 52, p. 128.

118. Ibid, vol. 52, p. 129. citing from *Kamal al din* of Suduq

119. Ibid, vol. 52, p. 123 citing from *Kamal al din* of Suduq

120. Ibid, vol. 52, p. 140 citing from *Al-Ghayba* of al-Nu'mani

121. Sharif Razi, *Nahjul Balagha*, Sermon 138.

122. Majlisi, *Bihar al-anwar*, (Beirut: Mu'sassat al-Wafa', n.d.), vol. 52, p. 140 citing from *Al-Ghayba* of al-Nu'mani

www.ingramcontent.com/pod-product-compliance
Lightning Source LLC
Chambersburg PA
CBHW030304100526
44590CB00012B/515